MW01232557

The Book of
Balanced Living

The Book of Balanced Living

Options to take control of your time, work and life

Lucy McCarraher and Lucy Daniels

First published in 2002 by
Spiro Press
17–19 Rochester Row
London
SW1P 1LA
Telephone: +44 (0)870 400 1000

© Lucy McCarraher and Lucy Daniels 2002

© Typographical arrangement Spiro Press 2002

ISBN 1 904298 09 5

Reprint 2002
Ref 6105.JC.11.02

British Library Cataloguing-in-Publication Data.
A catalogue record for this book is available from the British Library.

All rights reserved. No part of this publication may be reproduced, stored in a retrieval
system or transmitted, in any form or by an means, electronic, mechanical, photocopying,
recording and/or otherwise without the prior written permission of the publishers. This
book may not be lent, resold, hired out or otherwise disposed of by way of trade in any
form, binding or cover other than that in which it is published without the prior written
consent of the publishers.

Spiro Press USA
3 Front Street, Suite 331
PO Box 338
Rollinsford NH 03869
USA

Typeset by: Q3 Bookwork, Loughborough
Printed in Great Britain by: JW Arrowsmith Ltd
Cover image by: Photodisc
Cover design by: Cachet Creatives

Contents

The Balance Model

Introduction

Do you feel under pressure at home and at work – always seeming to be in the wrong place at the wrong time, never quite managing to meet your commitments, always disappointing someone? Then this is the book for you. This is a book for people who want to take more control of their time, work and life (while recognizing that work *is* part of life). It is for people who want to create a better balance for themselves, and those around them. Bristling with practical advice and real-life insights, this user-friendly book will help you assess the possibilities and practicalities of change. From rearranging your hours to re-organizing your household, this book brings together the options, helping you to decide on your next move.

Whether under the guise of 'family-friendly employment', 'work-life integration' or 'time sovereignty', balancing work and home has been a major concern for those with caring responsibilities for decades. Recent changes in society, employment and the workplace, though, have led everyone to consider how to manage the demands of work alongside home. We want greater freedom of choice about where and how we live and to concentrate on what we most value in life. Younger people, especially, want a better work-life balance than they saw their parents struggling with.

Some of the more obvious trends that have triggered these issues include: a faster pace in work (driven by information technology);

downsizing and global competition; a move away from the expectation of a job for life; the growth in single person households and the rising number of families in which both parents are working, and our extended life expectancy.

Some employers have taken on board the need to offer greater flexibility in order to attract and retain employees; others have been less far-sighted. Yet, even in more innovative organizations there are many people who find today's sheer volume of work makes it a struggle to keep up with their commitments. While there is much that employers can do to foster an environment in which it is OK to talk about these issues, it is also down to you as an individual to negotiate the balance that works for you. This is particularly true of the growing numbers of self-employed, contractors and others who don't have access to corporate work-life policies. For you, reliance on your personal ability to navigate work-life issues is vital. And then there are those of you who are not currently employed – whether out of choice, life-stage or because you are looking for work – but still need to bring a better balance into your lives.

We hope this book will be a useful tool for all of you: for women and men; single people, those in partnerships and family carers; from students to the retired; from senior managers to those on the shop floor and the majority of people between the two. It's equally relevant whether you live to work or work to live; for people whose interests include community, education, sports, pets and a social life as well as those with caring responsibilities.

Regardless of your stage in life, *The Book of Balanced Living* will provide you with some simple formulae for assessing your current aspirations in terms of your career, well-being, lifelong learning and relationships.

It will show you how to go about finding the right answers to your questions and offers guidance and practical tools to empower you to realize your goals. Our approach is an holistic one, and we hope to help you gain an insight into your individual relationship to your work and home life, and offer strategies to bring about positive change. This book cannot provide all the answers, but it will outline your options and point you in the right direction.

- In Chapter 1 we look at some of the background issues which shape our attitudes to work and home, and the changing ways we need to find balance as we move through lifecycle stages.

- In Chapter 2 you can check out how your work and home roles define your identity, the relationship between your work and life, and the financial and emotional investments you've made in both.

- We get down to practicalities in Chapter 3, looking at what work has to provide to meet both your material and emotional needs. If it's not doing both, it may be time to make some changes.

- You can make significant adjustments in your current working life, and in Chapter 4 we show you how – from better time and workload management to a more organized home. There are also options for changing your working arrangements; we outline the choices and show you how to get your boss to agree to them!

- If you've discovered (or decided) that radical change is required, Chapter 5 tells you how to find the work you'll love, and either an employer who'll pay you to do it or how to set up on your own.

- Finally, in Chapter 6, we round up practical ways you can deal with other work-life issues, from stress and health problems to childcare.

How to use this book

There are various ways in which this book can help you balance the different elements of your life. If you're already aware of the issues you want to deal with, and are looking for some strategies to apply, you could pick out certain chapters, read the case studies of people who have been in a similar position and look at our suggestions of how to move on from there. For example, if you are happy in your job, but want to know how best to approach your manager about more flexibility, Chapter 4 may give you all the ideas you need to take things forward. If you already know that your future path is through self-employment, some of Chapter 5 will give you useful tips about how to achieve this.

Maybe you're coming up to a new challenge, such as moving from education into the job market, starting a family, returning to work after time off, or looking towards retirement or slowing down. Reading through *The Book of Balanced Living* at your own pace, doing the exercises that seem relevant to you and allowing yourself time to work through some of the options and ideas that we, or other people's experience, suggest, should prove a useful exercise.

If, on the other hand, you feel there is a more significant imbalance in your life, and that it is related to either or both of your work and home life, you may want to use the book as more of a short study course. Take one chapter at a time and give yourself at least a week to read the text and case studies and complete the suggested exercises before moving on to the next. Some of the issues we touch upon can connect with long-term and very personal attitudes and experiences, which may take time to explore.

An important tool in this book is the 'Balance Model'. The seven exercises related to this are spread throughout Chapters 2-5, but you can work through them as a single activity if you wish (see Contents page for listings).

Two of the most useful tools you can use to bringing balance into your life are a hardback A4 notebook and a good pen. This is your 'Balance Book', dedicated to improving your work-life balance. As you read through *The Book of Balanced Living* make notes of your thoughts and reactions in your Balance Book. Also use it to complete the extended exercises. There is no reason why you shouldn't do this on a PC or laptop, but you may find that taking your Balance Book around with you, and writing down memories, ideas, notes and reminders for action that occur to you, is very useful.

We have also found that spending from 10 minutes to half an hour simply writing down whatever comes into your head first thing in the morning can be an excellent way of capturing revelations and connections that your subconscious has been processing overnight. Writing down anxieties that wake you in the night can also be a helpful way of dealing with them and getting back to sleep, knowing you can use the notes in your Balance Book as a prompt for action in the morning.

If you do keep a Balance Book, don't look back over what you've written too often; leave it until you have finished working on the chapter in hand before revisiting your notes. You're not writing literature and your Balance Book should be entirely *private to you*, so only you need to know what your notes, scribbles and even drawings or diagrams mean.

Alternatively, if writing isn't the way you stimulate or relax your brain, try meditating, or simply sitting quietly at least once a day, preferably first thing in the morning. Try to think of nothing in particular, for a minimum of 10 minutes, perhaps concentrating on your own breathing, a part of your body or a sound in your head. Wait and see what intuitions bubble up into your conscious, but resting, mind that suggest new directions you might want to follow.

However you choose to use this book, we hope that our experiences, insights and suggestions – and those of the other people who appear as our case studies – will at the least give you some fresh ideas of achieving a better balance between your work and home life, and at the most give you the tools to change your life for the better, for good!

Throughout the book you'll find the stories of individuals looking for balance. Some of these are people who have allowed us to use their own words about their personal experiences. Others are based on real people we have worked with, but whose experiences we have combined or edited to provide the most helpful and varied examples. We follow the experiences of these real-life 'characters' throughout the book, seeing how they face up to the work-life challenge.

All case studies appear in plain, indented 'sans serif' type. Names and many identifying details have been changed.

CHAPTER 1

Why you, why now?

THIS CHAPTER CONSIDERS:

- Perceptions of work and home life – the cultural, social, historical and political context.

- What are your hidden influences?

- Work-life balance – the new agenda: changing demographics.

- The workforce of the future.

- Lifecycle stages – starting out, settling down, young families, the sandwich years, moving on.

- Where are you now and what are your issues?

Perceptions of work and home

You probably grew up learning that, in due course, paid employment would become an essential part of your life. Probably one or both of your parents and other adults around you went to work and told you something of what they did in the time they were away. Your education at home and at school was largely about preparing you to take your place in society as an emotionally and financially independent person. If not, perhaps you grew up in a very wealthy household or lived with long-term unemployed parents where lack of jobs made the situation seem normal. Or perhaps, as a woman in your late 50s or older, you were brought up on the idea that a woman's place is in the home caring for her family. The rest of us have almost certainly been brought up to see 'work' and 'home' as the defining axes on which our lives are aligned.

Your own, individual attitude to the relationship between these two areas of life will have been formed from different but interrelated factors, including many you're aware of – such as family background, country of origin, religious/cultural beliefs and your educational experience – and many you are unaware of. Many of the influences on your perceptions have evolved outside your own experience, either historically or in a wider cultural context during your lifetime. Some of the following approaches and movements may have fed into your understanding of your own work-life balance.

Attitudes to work and home – a brief history

In the Middle Ages, for most people in most parts of the world, work was about survival. Men, women and children all played their part and what happened at home was part of the process rather than a separate sphere. Life was lived on a collective basis for all ages and classes, and few people had the time – or space – at home for solitude and privacy. Nor was the concept of 'family' imbued with the emotional resonance it carries today; the family simply provided a means of continuity of life, property and names. Medieval society had little idea of education for the masses and therefore childhood was as brief as the human weaning period could be (usually about seven years), after which children went straight into the shared community of adult work.

The Jesuits' famous edict, "Give me a child until he is seven and I will give you the man", was revolutionary in the 16th century, as previously all teaching had been addressed to adults. In directing their writings and propaganda towards children and young people, they also taught parents that they were the spiritual guardians of their children and responsible for their souls – and bodies – before God. Due to this influence, it gradually became accepted that children were not ready for life at such an early age and needed to undergo a longer time of protection before they were allowed to join the adult world. The longer and more judicious care and education of children introduced an initial separation between the worlds of paid work and home, as it forced some adults, too, to stay in the home with children for longer than before.

A century or so later, the Industrial Revolution caused another division, as many families migrated from the countryside into towns to take up jobs in the new manufacturing industries. Suddenly work was no longer a regional, seasonal and communal activity, dictated by where you lived and in which each individual's contribution was for the good of the group. Now employment had to be located, competed for, travelled to and economically viable in terms of maintaining a personal, separate life away from the workplace.

Cultural influences

Your country of origin and that of your parents, as well as your religious background (practising or otherwise), will have had an effect on how you see yourself and on your attitudes towards men's and women's roles at work and home. Many cultures and religions have contributed to the influences on society, but one that has persisted in the Western world came from 16th century Swiss reformer, John Calvin. What became known as the 'Protestant work ethic' spread through the whole of Western Europe and was carried to the new world of America by its Protestant settlers, the Pilgrim Fathers. This belief that work is good for the soul of both individuals and society in general has been more pervasive and longer standing than any other part of the movement that produced it, and is reflected in much current employment legislation, particularly in Europe and the UK.

Anthony, 52, middle manager

Anthony had worked for (a major bank) since leaving school at 16. He had worked his way up the organization and was planning on staying until he could afford to retire, perhaps early with luck, on a reasonable pension. Unfortunately, the last couple of years had seen a lot of organizational change. At the same time, with his children growing up and leaving school, his wife Della had taken the opportunity to get involved in some new activities for herself, which Anthony felt excluded from.

"We'd always agreed that I earned the money and she looked after the family, but that's changing now and it feels odd not having her home. It's all change at the bank too. They expect me to work with a laptop, but I thought it was just a passing fad and didn't really pay much attention to the training course. It turns out they expect me to visit clients whenever they ask me; I feel like I've become a glorified salesman for the bank's financial products."

Anthony was managing by telling clients that his laptop had problems, going back to the office and working late doing calculations by hand and sending them contracts on by post. "And they're cutting back jobs for managers at my level, and I'm hardly in a good position to hold on to mine. If I don't make it into the next round, I could be made redundant with a small lump sum, and I can't access my pension for another seven years."

Anthony had become bad tempered at home and resentful of his children, Rob and Lisa, who had left full-time education but were still living at home. He admitted to drinking more in the evening, which didn't help concentration at work the next day, and he had been getting chest pains. "Where has it all gone wrong? This is not what I expected from life but it all seems beyond my control. If I can just keep my head above water maybe things will work out in the end."

Gender, work and home

Eventually, these major social movements produced a formal separation between men and women. In the late 18th century, work was seen as the morally appropriate environment for men as was the home for women. It wasn't until after the Second World War, during which women had, of necessity, stepped into men's work boots, that it became clear that women were equal to most activities which had previously been considered 'men's work'. The unhappiness of women confined to the home once more, after the men had returned from war, was described by Betty Friedan in her book, *The Feminine Mystique,* published in 1963. Their problem, which she termed "mystique", was called "oppression" by later feminist writers; but Friedan opened the door to a woman's right to fulfilment other than as a wife and mother.

Despite entrenched resistance by some men – and indeed women – to this idea, women have made huge strides in the workplace, although pay inequalities still exist. Interestingly, the process of including equal numbers of men in some traditionally female areas of work, such as paid and unpaid domestic service and childcare, continues to be a slow one.

Della, 48, entering a new phase

Della and Anthony married young. He was doing well at the bank and she always planned to give up her secretarial work when they had children. When their youngest, Rob, started school, Della took a part-time receptionist job for a local real estate company and was still there 14 years later. "The extra money comes in handy and it gets me out of the house. But actually I really enjoy my working days, and when I saw what the sales people were doing, I often thought I could do their job just as well. But they all worked full time and put in really long hours, and I couldn't look after the children and Anthony if I was doing that, so I just stayed put on reception."

Della now wanted to do more with her life outside the home, but she also had the responsibility for helping Anthony's increasingly frail parents, who lived nearby. They relied on her to pop in regularly, do heavy grocery shopping and generally be on hand. She was all too aware that they were going to become more dependent over the next few years.

She had started evening classes in yoga and interior design, but wasn't confident that she had the right experience to find more interesting and flexible work. "Maybe I've left it too late and no one will want to employ a housewife with only a bit of reception experience. And I am anxious about Anthony's work and the stress he's under. He won't admit he's got problems – I wish he'd talk to me, perhaps I could help him. And Rob and Lisa may be grown up, but they don't get any tidier or more responsible around the house. I suppose that's kids for you."

Pressure on parents

Parents today are expected to be as professional in bringing up their children as they are in their career. This 'professionalization' of parenting started in the 1950s, with experts like John Bowlby claiming that children could suffer serious emotional problems if their early relationship with their biological mother was broken. Dr Spock's *Common Sense Book of Baby and Child Care* was highly influential in the move towards liberal, child-centred methods of baby-care, and the behaviourist, Jean Piaget, suggested that parents should stimulate their children at defined stages of development to release their full potential.

The pressure on mothers, in particular, to be doing the 'right' thing for their children hasn't let up since the 50s, while the possibilities of doing the 'wrong' things seem to multiply. This was the first time the blame for children's 'bad' or unacceptable behaviour was returned squarely to the parents. Professor RM Titmuss was right when he predicted that "Society is in the process of making parenthood a highly self-conscious, self-regarding affair. In doing so it is adding heavily to the sense of personal responsibility among parents. Their tasks are much harder and involve more risks of failure when children have to be brought up as individual successes in a supposedly mobile, individualistic society …"

Karen, 36, returning to work

Karen had been a full-time mother for five years; her son Paul was at full-time school and daughter Kylie about to start half-day pre-school. Karen had always planned to find part-time work when both children were in full-time school, but was having to think about moving more quickly. Her relationship with Dave, her partner of 10 years, was going through a rocky patch and they had financial problems with a high interest loan for a new car and an expensive holiday "that I wish we'd never taken". Karen wondered whether Dave was having an affair; "He's never around and I'm sick of telling the kids he's at work." She was preparing mentally for the possibility that she and Dave might split up, and coming to realize that his wage wouldn't support two households.

Before she had children Karen had worked in catering, which she loved; but restaurant hours wouldn't allow her to collect her children from school and she hadn't seen any appropriate part-time jobs advertised. "If I could bring some money into the family it might make things better with Dave; and if he leaves I'll have to work anyway. I do look for part-time jobs but there's nothing around in catering and I don't know what else I can do. I've tried to do my bit as full-time wife and mum, but to be honest it's been hard and I don't think Dave's pulled his weight at home. Perhaps I should have stayed working all along."

Fatherhood revisited

Although throughout the 1970s and 80s women moved into the employment market, they generally didn't reject their mothering role. Many of the generation of working mothers who were supposed to be 'having it all' simply ended up 'doing it all' – work, childcare, household chores. Some feminists hoped that men's involvement in childcare would both shift the balance of power and redefine the activity as "creative, worthy, responsible and high status" (Dale Spender in *For the Record*, 1985), and by the 1980s there had been a slight shift in this direction. The media helped by portraying working couples with perfect children as the acme of success. Advertisements for a range of fashionable products were sold on the images of caring fathers who were both breadwinners and (sometimes inept) participators in their children's upbringing. In fact, the press was only reflecting a genuine trend in which a new generation of dads were choosing to be different from their own, more remote, fathers and sharing some of the pleasures and pressures of childcare with their partners. At the same time, men's jobs were no longer necessarily providing them with lifelong employment, security, status or a social life. Family life was a way of achieving relaxation for the over-stressed, and continuity and support for the under- or unemployed.

Even today, however, mothers are still considered to be the key figures in their children's early lives and reports on the adverse affects on children from mothers in full-time employment still surface with regularity. Legislation and many employers continue to prioritize women's rights to flexible and part-time working around childcare issues, though challenges to this gender-based inequality are gaining momentum.

Dave, 38, long-hours worker

Dave admitted he had wanted Karen to give up work when they had children, but didn't feel she appreciated how hard he'd worked to keep the family income up to their previously dual-earner level. "I know she thought I should have done more with the children, but when you work four 12-hour shifts … OK, you have four days off, but two of those are recovering from the last shift and one's getting ready to go back in again." Dave had thought buying a new car and taking an expensive holiday would make Karen feel better about her home-bound life, but the loan repayments had turned out to be more than they could manage. Even so, Dave's impression of their relationship problems was much less pessimistic than Karen's: "We're not getting on very well at the moment but it's not serious; we'd never split up. Karen worries too much, it'll blow over. We do need the money to pay off the loan, but sometimes I work the overtime to stay out of the house. And sometimes I go for a drink with the lads after work rather than go home and face another row. Karen will calm down if I stay out of her way for a bit."

Beer and sandwiches

The postwar baby-boomers are the largest population bulge of the 20th/21st centuries and those born between, say, 1945 and 1960 form the most influential group, perhaps ever. Many of us (speaking as two of them) are now finding ourselves in the position of becoming responsible for the needs of our parents, older friends and relatives who, like us all, are living longer than previous generations. These demands often occur while our children are staying on longer in the family home. Hence we are becoming known as the 'sandwich generation', those who find themselves as the meat in the proverbial snack, pressed into caring service by both our children and parents at the same time.

We baby-boomers are also the most divorced and separated group ever, and have stood up for the rights of those who are not in partnerships, families or caring relationships. What the media have called a "backlash" against rights for parents and carers from single people is in fact a natural extension of the demand for recognition of a life outside of work for men and women at all ages and stages of life. The young, the single, those in alternative relationships or with alternative lifestyles, older people in a caring hiatus – all should now be seen as having the right to be able to find balance in their lives between work and other activities.

Marie, 43, director of human resources (HR)

Marie was the HR director of a city council which employed around 3,000 people in a variety of employment, from a call centre dealing with enquiries and complaints from the public to staff working on housing projects, libraries, roads, parks and other public amenities. She was single and dedicated to her career: "I'm proud of my work here, I've introduced a range of innovative working policies and practices in the face of opposition from some of the directors. I hope that I show a caring attitude towards the staff; I operate an 'open door' policy, and I'm pleased to say that lots of people take advantage of this to ask my advice on their problems both at work and at home."

But now Marie felt she had reached a plateau. Although she was still enjoying her work, she had recently found life less fulfilling than she'd expected at this stage. She knew she could earn more in the corporate sector, but didn't need any more money. She had a nice home, a good car and took golfing holidays with friends two or three times a year – but still she found herself taking work home in the evening "because it's the most interesting thing I do".

Marie knew she could always spend more time with her brothers who both had children – although she saw them all often, and her parents were in good health. "I do enjoy my freedom, but I feel I need a change of direction or a break – or to give something back to the community."

Current attitudes

Today, in the early years of the 21st century, we generally assume that most people want to work in paid employment, not just from necessity but to fund a lifestyle of reasonable quality, for the interest or ambition of pursuing a career, or perhaps to make a contribution to society. We also accept that, for many different reasons, many of us will want to take time out from earning a living for periods of time, whether to care for others (children or dependent adults), for personal refreshment, for education or to take part in other interests. But we still believe that between finishing our formal education and reaching the age of either statutory or chosen 'retirement', most of us will want, when at all possible, to work for our living. The world of work itself, though, is changing, and it is doing so faster now than at any other time in the history of civilization.

The emergence of choice

While most people value the role and status that work accords them, First World expectations of quality of life outside work have risen enormously over the last 50 years. This is due to a powerful combination of the universal availability of better education and healthcare, the flattening of social structures and rise of disposable income, the development of communications technology and media reportage, the regulation of working hours and conditions, and the development of 'labour saving' domestic technology along with fast, affordable travel and wide-ranging leisure activities. Advances in psychology, psychiatry and support professions such as counselling have also contributed to our belief that we can all achieve a fulfilling and contented existence. Small wonder then that for many of us not being able to achieve the perfect balance between a stimulating career, positive family and social relationships, and a range of interests, can seem like inexplicable failure.

Jonathan, 28, caring for others

Jonathan had always wanted to be a geriatric nurse and the reality of his work hadn't changed that. He worked in a public hospital and found that caring for the patients made all the staff and money shortages bearable. "It's not good pay, though. I can just about manage to rent my own apartment and, with another set of exams under my belt, I'll get promotion and a bit of a pay rise." Jonathan's problem with his job was the long shifts he worked and last-minute changes, which made studying and attending classes extremely difficult.

Worse than that, he thought he might have to re-home Max, his much loved terrier, because of the long and unpredictable hours. "At the moment I have to rely on my neighbour to walk and feed Max when I can't, but the amount of help I'm asking her for is going way over the top. It's so embarrassing, but I can't afford to pay a professional dog-walker."

Jonathan had become resentful of constantly covering for nurses with families who were allowed to take first choice of shifts and assumed that he could cover for them when they had childcare problems. "For me, Max is like family and my studies are really important to me. I'm gay, so it's unlikely I'll ever have children myself, so it's not even a case of waiting until it's my turn for special treatment."

Jonathan was regularly waking up with anxiety and felt constant guilt at work about Max being shut up in the apartment all day. "But I can't talk to my colleagues or my boss about it – they'll just think I'm stupid to worry so much about a dog, and probably that I'm selfish about wanting to study and get on."

Exercise

What are your hidden influences?

It is useful to consider the influences on your own attitudes towards paid employment and life outside work. Take a few minutes to work out whether your childhood and background provided you with generally positive or negative feelings about work and home.

Tick a 'Positive', 'Neutral' or 'Negative' box on the form overleaf to indicate how you feel your early influences affected your attitude towards work and home. Do this quickly, using instant, intuitive responses rather than reasoned thought processes.

INFLUENCE	PAID WORK			TIME AT HOME		
	Positive	Neutral	Negative	Positive	Neutral	Negative
Mother (or female role model)						
Father (or male role model)						
Extended family						
Close family friends						
Religion or culture						
Community or neighbourhood						
School/teachers						
Friends						
Books/magazines you used to read						
TV programmes watched						
Other significant influences – as many as relevant						
TOTAL:						

Add up the total number of ticks in each column. Now see whether you recall your early/background influences as mainly positive, neutral or negative. Which area was seen as the more important overall – work or home? Does this coincide with your current attitudes to work and home and has this exercise raised any memories or connections which might be affecting your perception of your own work-life balance?

In your Balance Book, take this intuitive exercise a little further. Under each 'Influence' heading, write down as many words or phrases as occur to you in relation to work and home as you can. For example, you might start with:

MOTHER

Work – part-time, pin money, community, voluntary, financially dependent, status reflected from dad, gives him the right to be cared for, not her place, not qualified, scared of …

Home – where she belongs, children, cooking, caring, busy, house-proud, needed, comfort zone, friends, family, enjoys entertaining, feels secure, frustrated?

FATHER

Work – breadwinner, status, money, unfulfilled ambitions, really wanted to study medicine but couldn't afford fees, looking forward to retirement, stressed but feels it's his world, golf …

Home – proud of house and garden, golf higher priority than children? Finds it hard to unwind from work, but fun when does relax, enjoys entertaining (but often work colleagues), thinks it's a woman's world, defers to mum …

Work through the headings from the form opposite and when you have completed those, or those which you consider most relevant, write a new heading – 'ME'.

Without stopping to think, write as much as you can about your own feelings, attitudes and connections with your work and then your home life. Again, use single words or phrases with meaning to you – they don't have to make sense to anyone else.

When you have finished, compare what you have written under 'ME' with what you've written under the other headings. Try to see connections and references to where some of your attitudes originated. Try to see which influences you have accepted, and which you have rebelled against.

Are you following in, or working hard *not* to follow in, the footsteps of one or both of your parents? Are you still trying to prove yourself to one of them or to a teacher who had high or low expectations of you? Give yourself time for both your subconscious and conscious mind to work through the answers to these questions.

Work-life balance – the new agenda

Workplace arrangements to help people with caring responsibilities balance work with family life (generally known as 'family friendly' policies) started developing in a number of organizations in the 1980s. These followed over a decade of initiatives which aimed to advance the status of women and addressed equality and fairness in the workplace. It became increasingly clear, though, that women could not compartmentalize their lives outside work, nor could their employers ignore them, and that their need to balance domestic responsibilities and childcare had to be recognized.

Some of the earliest initiatives were developed in Nordic countries. They were driven by a combination of post-war labour shortages and equal opportunities legislation, reinforced with a strong sense of collective social responsibility. Elsewhere, many organizations began to develop policies even in the absence of government support. By the early 1990s, numerous companies had embraced a range of work and family policies and programmes. These efforts marked an important first step in helping employees – particularly mothers of young children – to balance work and home responsibilities.

The most significant advances were made in large, public sector organizations as well as in big businesses with a high proportion of female staff. In these sectors a wide range of policies and practices now exist, including flexible working options, leave for family reasons and dependant care support. These organizations recognized the business rationale for developing policies that helped cut staff turnover and its associated costs in terms of recruitment, training and productivity, and which helped build employee morale and commitment.

Changing demographics

While change in the workplace has accelerated since the 1990s, the culture and composition of families has also undergone fundamental change. One of the major changes has been the demise of the male breadwinner. 'Traditional' family patterns have been superseded by a variety of new ones, including a massive rise in single parent families.

In the UK:

- One in five of all families is headed by a lone parent, 10% of whom are fathers.

- An estimated 2.4 million men are carers.

- The proportion of 'traditional' (a couple with dependent children) family households has fallen from 38% of all UK households in 1961 to 25% in 1996–97.

- In 1996–97 couples with no children (28%) outnumbered those with dependent children (26%).

- The population is ageing: long-term projections indicate that the number of over 65s will peak during the 2030s (the baby-boomer effect again!), and in affluent societies there will be more older dependent people than under 16s for the first time in 2008.

These figures are similar in most Western countries, including Europe, the US, Canada and Australia.

'Family friendly' working is now recognized as an issue that concerns fathers as much as mothers, but the use of this term still reinforces the idea that such policies are just for working parents with young children. In fact, choice, control and flexibility in working conditions and personal fulfillment outside work is equally important to young workers, single people and couples, older employees and those whose relationships and families do not fall into conventional patterns. Hence the more recent and inclusive term 'work-life balance', which puts the issue of employee well-being at the core of business strategy and doesn't discriminate between those 'deserving' such consideration, such as parents and carers, and others.

The workforce of the future

Research now shows conclusively that employers whose workforce is able to achieve a healthy balance between work and home are more productive, retain their staff for longer, attract more and higher quality recruits to their organization, experience less sickness and absence, and record higher levels of morale and commitment. The following statistics, taken from a variety of recent, significant surveys, give you an idea of why this is the case. Although mostly UK in origin, they reflect trends in other Western countries.

Young people

- 45% of business students worldwide consider achieving work-life balance a top future priority.

- Work-life balance for leisure and skills development is considered more important than work-family issues, but a good job with financial stability is still a priority.

- 50% of young singles would like a year's unpaid leave.

- 90% of 12–25 year olds say men and women should take equal responsibility for children.

- Men under 35 are more likely to do domestic chores.

Lisa, 22, starting out

Lisa (the daughter of Anthony and Della) had a degree in media studies and was ambitious and smart. But it was tough having to start at the bottom of this very competitive industry. As a production assistant she had to work long hours for low pay, around complex shooting schedules. She was disappointed, in her first job after college, to find herself assigned to the most lowly office jobs with little chance of using, let alone developing, the skills she had learned at college. She was also finding living at home again restricting, after sharing a flat while she was a student, but couldn't afford to share a place with friends in better paid employment. "I don't envy them, it sounds really boring working in banks and insurance. But although film and TV sounds glamorous, if they knew how I spent my days they'd laugh. Still, I suppose I am learning. But my social life's rubbish too because I'm working such long hours; I've got no money and I'm living at home."

Lisa's real ambition was to travel, and she thought that would come from working with a company that made travel documentaries. Now she was thinking of leaving, but hadn't any clear plans of when or what else she could do. "A job like this was my idea of heaven – I didn't think it would mean being stuck in an office typing up scripts, doing the photocopying and making coffee while the crews jet off round the world. I'm also really worried about ending up as some kind of secretary – the last thing I want is to end up like my mother, with no proper career other than being a housekeeper to my dad."

Families

Young people are starting families later, which means women are usually higher up the career ladder when they take maternity leave. Employers have a greater investment in such employees – including experience, training and seniority – because:

• Over 40% of births are now to women in their 30s.

• 64%, and rising, of couples with dependent children both work.

• Two out of three women now return to work within 11 months of the birth of a child, but more return to work with employers who offer flexible and part-time hours.

• British fathers work the longest hours in Europe; one in four works over 50 hours per week.

• Only 17% of men work shorter hours after having children, but demands from fathers for flexibility are becoming stronger.

Managers

Employers are having to look at the terms and conditions of work of their most valued employees, and the costs of losing them to competitors.

- Only 12% of managers now describe work as more important than home.

- 59% say long hours reduces their productivity.

- 65% say it damages their health.

- 79% say it leaves no time for other interests.

- 72% say it affects their relationship with their partner.

- An estimated 30% of sick leave is related to stress, anxiety and depression.

Lifecycle stages and issues

Although our wider range of options – from society, our employers and our own attitudes – must be an improvement on the comparatively limited lives previous generations led, the amount of choice we now have in organizing our lives can be a pressure in itself. The alternatives we have, though, are different at different stages of the lifecycle, and each has its own in-built limitations. Most people's life-stages, and the work-life balance issues that are likely to arise in each, fall into the following broad categories.

Starting out

When you leave education – whether school or college, and regardless of the qualifications you have achieved – finding a first job, leaving home and learning emotional, financial and domestic self-reliance are major life transitions. Whether you are single or in a relationship, at this stage of your life you are likely to be making decisions mainly for yourself rather than for a family. This doesn't necessarily make the decisions any easier as, depending on where you live and what sort of work you are looking for, the choices may be incomprehensibly wide or frustratingly limited. When you find paid employment, the hours, the role and the skills you will be required to fulfil are all likely to be very different from what you have experienced before in the world of education or vacation jobs. At the same time as negotiating these new parameters and proving your worth to your boss and work colleagues, you are having to learn to live to a budget on your wages, probably pay for travel to and lunches at work, appropriate clothes and perhaps equipment. This may be the time when you are moving into a place of your own, or alternatively contributing to the family home, which involves both financial and domestic responsibilities.

Rob, 19, sports enthusiast

Rob left school at 16 without many qualifications. He felt he had been a bit of a disappointment to his parents (Anthony and Della), particularly after Lisa's academic success. He wasn't thinking in terms of a career yet, but took on casual jobs when he needed the money and left when he was bored. "I've worked stacking shelves, on an assembly line, answering phones … I'm into sport – that's what I live for. I follow all sports and play soccer for my local club." Rob was in the first team at school and had been told by his coach that if he worked at it he could become a professional; but he didn't have the self-confidence to pursue it. "I did talk about going for it, but it was more of an excuse not to look for any other job. I think I could still do it if I found the right coach to push me, but … What else? I hang out with my mates, listen to music, go clubbing on the weekend. If I've got enough money to do that, I'm sorted."

But Rob had just started dating a new girlfriend, and she had a good job and was encouraging him to do more with his life. Rob thought it could be his first serious relationship, and that he should do something to make her think he was worth being with. Rob had always been good at computer games and had done some programming on his own – perhaps this could be an area to pursue? But he was ambivalent about what a 'real job' or career might mean: "If I get a proper job does that mean getting stuck in one place for the rest of my life, like dad? And what's he got to show for it? He can't even work his laptop, although I could show him if he'd listen to me."

Settling down

Typically, you will 'settle down' sometime in your 20s or early 30s. This will generally see you becoming established in a career, finding a long-term partner whom you may marry, moving into a new and better home – either as a single person or a couple – rather than sharing with a group of friends. You are now likely to take on more financial commitments, including a car, mortgage, insurance policies, savings schemes and a pension. During this stage, men and women may well put in long hours for both financial reasons and to build a career. You may also undertake further training or education, either to move your career forward or for personal interest, spend money on holidays and travel and buy more consumer items to furnish your home. Towards the end of this stage you may be planning for and starting a family, or considering some other major change in your life such as relocation, starting a business or changing direction in other ways.

Ed, 32, IT consultant

Ed said he was an only, and a bit of a lonely, child and that there was nothing he wanted more than to have a couple of kids and a home with a warm, family atmosphere. He was employed by a global IT company who hired him out as a consultant to other businesses, selling, installing and supporting software products in clients' sites. His work took him around the country and it was normal for him to spend two or three nights a week away from home. "I've got used to this sort of life, and Naomi's working long hours at the moment, but I don't want to do it for much longer. I want to settle down, for us to become a family and for my life to revolve around that."

Ed recognized that his current employer offered good benefits and allowed him some flexibility, such as working a day a week from home on administration if client needs allowed. But he wasn't planning to stay with them for more than another year at the most: "My plan, which I haven't told Naomi yet, is to start my own consultancy business with some colleagues. Perhaps a virtual organization, with everyone working from home, or from client offices, connected by high-powered communications systems." He knew that the first year would be tough, as the business and its clients were developed, but thought that if it was successful he would be able to take it easy, project manage from a distance and be more flexible with the hours he could work. He wanted to be able to do his share of the childcare.

"I was planning to tell Naomi about my ideas when we got news that her mother was seriously ill. It didn't seem the right time to come out with my business plans, so I thought I'd wait until she'd decided what to do about that. I'm not sure what she'll think when I tell her we'll need to move to a bigger house to accommodate my home office."

Young families

If you are a couple with small children, typically if you are in your late 20s and 30s (although this lifecycle stage is continuing to start and finish later for many people), you might be finding life tough. In over 60% of cases, both of you will be in paid employment, but far more mothers than fathers will be working part-time and flexibly to accommodate childcare and school hours. Many women now return to the workplace before the children are school age, with childcare management taking up time and headspace both at home and at work. Reconciling childcare arrangements for young children of different ages can often be problematic until they are all in full-time school – although transitions continue to prove difficult and siblings are often at different schools.

Although more fathers are taking on a house-husband role or equal share in the balancing act between work and home responsibilities, men are still more likely to be filling the gaps, such as dropping off at, or collecting from, nursery/childminding/school, rather than taking full responsibility for childcare.

Daniel, neurosurgeon, father of three

"Balancing my life? What with going to Bangladesh next week to do some relief work, writing up my MD thesis, studying for my final neurosurgical exit exam, speaking at four international conferences, Amsterdam, London, Cairns and Sydney, and father of three … I don't need a book, I need a clone! But seriously, I have to think about balance in very long-term spans. It's not on a weekly, or even monthly, basis. There have been long periods in my life, when I've been working towards exams or doing a piece of research, when I have put work demands before family needs. It doesn't necessarily make me popular at home, but I figure the more I can do to move my career forward now, the more money we'll have as a family and the more control I'll have over my time sooner. And already, as a consultant, I do less 'on call' weekends and evenings than I used to. My wife does understand (mostly) as she's in the medical profession too, but it is a very tough career to balance with a young family."

The majority of men in their 30s still see their most important contribution as that of family breadwinner, and indeed the costs of raising children are high, whether childcare, education and healthcare is subsidized by government or not. The pressures from peer groups and the media for the latest clothes and toys is intense upon children – and therefore on you, their parents, as providers. As parents you are also likely to be at the peak of your own financial commitments in paying for bigger houses and consumer items, while your income may be less than in pre-children days.

Inevitably these circumstances, combined with the pressures of work, can lead to stress and relationship problems, and this is the time when the highest number of separations and divorces occur. Part-time workers (usually women) often trade flexibility of hours for what works out as reduced pay – although not on a contractual basis. Most parents working reduced hours – and indeed their employers – say they tend to be more focused and productive than their full-time colleagues.

Naomi, 34, working for a multinational

Naomi, Ed's partner, was a senior research chemist in a multinational pharmaceutical company based at an out-of-town laboratory. She was dedicated to her work and had always put in long hours, partly because Ed did the same and partly to move up the career ladder. She had recently heard from her sister that their mother's latest illness had led to long-term problems and she might not live that long. Naomi wanted to take an extended break to see her mother, knowing it might be the last time, and she felt guilty that her sister was having to cope with all the caring because she had lived overseas since graduating. "But, and it's a big 'but' for me, I'm working on some crucial developments which, if they're successful, could result in the trialing and production of a new cancer drug. Of course, no one's indispensable, but I think my input is key and to take a break now would be like letting the whole team down. But more selfishly, it will be a vital step upwards in my career and at the moment every day of work counts. It's a horrible dilemma."

She was also feeling very stressed by Ed's enthusiasm for them to start a family. Naomi did want to have children, but wasn't sure they could manage family commitments alongside their careers right now. "I'm sure that as the woman it would end up being my career that has to be compromised and at the moment my career seems more important. And then there's the culture issue: if I have a child, I'd want him or her to grow up with an understanding of my culture, so I would want to take them back to my country for extended periods. If I had to go part-time as a mother, and also take some periods of extended time off, I wonder if I could really maintain my career path at all. Do professional women with careers and families really manage to juggle it all, or is it just one long series of compromises?"

The sandwich years

Men and women in their 40s and 50s are likely to be experiencing more changes at work than before and, if they have a family, probably a complete revision of the home situation with children growing up, leaving school and going into the job market directly or via tertiary education. A high proportion of people in this age group are single, whether long-term or following separation or divorce, and yet another group are with second or third long-term partners with whom they may or may not have children. There are also more and more women and men who have chosen to have children later in life and whose children are still young when they are in their 40s and early 50s.

For those of you whose children are less obviously dependent (although many young people are continuing to live longer at home) this period is a major life transition with important decisions to be made about the future. Some people of this age, who have worked through the raising of their families, will find themselves at the peak of their career and reaping financial and promotional rewards – but working long hours and dealing with stressful situations. Others, particularly men, may see this as a time when life can be taken a little easier, financial demands lessen, dreams that were shelved can be taken out and dusted off again to see if they might still be viable, and retirement looms as an agreeable long-term prospect. A number of women, on the other hand, who have put more time into their home than working lives, see this as a time to spread their career wings, shake off their caring responsibilities and return to an old career or invent a new way of life in which they can put their own needs and wishes first. A greater investment in personal and spiritual develop-ment is common.

However, for both sexes, for those who are single or in partnerships and for those who have grown up or still young children, the likelihood of eldercare responsibilities starting at this point in life is high. Parents and other relations are living into their 70s, 80s and beyond, they are becoming increasingly frail and needing to draw on the caring resources of their children to maintain the independent living that both parties see as desirable. Men are likely to take a more equal caring role in respect of their parents than they did with their children, but much of this eldercare work falls to sandwich generation women – limiting them once more in their choices of work-life balance.

Elizabeth, eldercare issues

"It was ironic that as a fundraising manager for a charity that promotes and supports the needs of carers, suddenly I found myself caring for three parents at once! My father was already in a residential nursing home as he has Alzheimer's disease. My husband and I suddenly found out that my mother-in-law, who is 86, had advanced cancer and had known about it for a year. Within a week, my mother was found to have a large growth in her stomach which might have been cancerous.

"Every weekend was spent rushing here, rushing there, visiting respective parents – it was not a weekend, it was a nightmare. My mother-in-law, who has always been fiercely independent, could no longer do her own shopping, go and get her pension or pay her bills as she was quite weak while undergoing daily radiotherapy. All this had to be organized and took hours of hanging on phones, gross inefficiency from benefits departments, banks and councils. All of which added to my stress.

"On the work front, I was expanding my busy fundraising department from two to three, so at precisely this time the new worker needed a lot of support and management, which added to my stress. During work time, I had many calls from home: rushing an ambulance to my mother-in-law, arranging for a repeat prescription in an emergency. It seemed that because I worked for a charity I would know what to do! Every time my phone rang, I froze – what next? My memory went, I banged into things and dropped things. There was one day when one minor incident caused me to have a panic attack and I really felt I couldn't go on. My manager was very understanding and suggested I went home. Strangely enough, that was the last thing I wanted to do; somehow work was the only normality I had.

"Gradually, things have begun to get better – my mother-in-law finished her radiotherapy, my mother had her operation and has recovered; it was not cancer.

"How do you cope? I found that I had to keep my home clean and tidy or I really got stressed out. The old saying 'taking each day as it comes' is very valuable. One of the ways that most of us cope with everyday life is to look forward to something. A holiday, a dinner out with friends, things we take for granted. At a time like this you are too frightened to plan anything, in case it has to be cancelled and you are disappointed.

"I made a list of personal and work tasks every day, ticking them off as I completed them. As long as I did one important work task and one personal task every day I felt better. Guilt is a problem, you will always feel you haven't done enough. You have got to take control of your own life and have a bit of fun or you will get too stressed or unwell to help anyone. Most important is to try to complete all your tasks on one day of the weekend. For example, I do all the shopping and visit respective parents on a Saturday. Therefore, on a Sunday, we have all day to do what we want. We try to plan something, even if it is a long walk with a nice lunch at the end of it, or a visit to the cinema. You need at least one day to be free like you once were, and to enjoy yourself without guilt.

"I work for an organization that promotes carers' needs to employers; consequently they have been very supportive. However, you will find that it is vital to discuss the situation with your manager or employer. Most of the employers that we advise say they didn't know that their employee was juggling work and care and were very willing to help once they had found out. Many had wondered why their employee's work had deteriorated, or why they were late or had had a lot of time off. You will be surprised at how many will be supportive. After all, if you are a valuable employee it is more cost effective for them to help you continue to work than recruiting and training someone new."

Moving on

For most of the 20th century most people could see their paid employment as a fixed way of life, taking place between set hours from the age you took a job until the organizational or statutory retirement age. Although this is still the norm, this will have to change in the 21st century as the number of people over current retirement age increases against those of 'working' age. One estimate suggests that by 2050 up to half of the European population will be over 60 – if you're one of these, you may not be able simply to give up paid work because pension and savings funds won't be able to support you. From a personal health and welfare point of view, the dramatic change from full-time work to enforced retirement can often prove negative, and many people experience feelings of uselessness, of feeling 'on the scrap heap'; depression and physical illness often set in.

Individually, many of you are starting to change your own working patterns when your financial commitments have started to bottom out, with a view to taking it easier on your own terms. With changing family structures and increased life expectancy, these sorts of modifications could take place at any time, but are more likely to be financially viable when you're over the age of 40. At this stage, at whatever point it may occur in lifecycle terms, you are likely to want to expend less time and/or less stress on your paid work and more time learning new skills or activities, relaxing and increasingly supporting or caring for older or ailing partners, friends or relations.

Tom and Sarah, both 62, running a small business

Tom and his wife, Sarah, had been running an independent dry cleaning business for seven years, since Tom had been made redundant by the factory he'd worked at for 40 years. He had been a production manager and with his redundancy money they had bought Class Cleaners as a going concern. Till this point Tom had been the breadwinner and Sarah the homemaker, but they took on the new business jointly and have since had to work long hours to build up turnover and get new services going, such as contract dry cleaning work for local businesses. They inherited the staff with the business and now some of them were getting older, some were leaving to have children, retire themselves or just move on. Tom and Sarah found themselves covering difficult shifts and sickness absences – which were happening more and more often.

Sarah said: "We had planned to slow down over the next couple of years, sell the business when we're 65 and retire to spend more time with the grandchildren and do some travelling. Now we're wondering if we're ever going to be able to spend less time at work, let alone retire. It feels as if we never leave the shop; we just go home to sleep. Half the time we're not even eating properly, and at our age we can't go on like this. I'm worried about Tom's health – he's on medication for high blood pressure and I think all this is making him worse."

Tom said that he felt bad for Sarah because she was missing out on time with their young grandchildren, and he felt bad for his children who could use their mother's help with the kids. "I don't know what else we could have done when the factory closed. A lot of my friends got depressed and didn't find other jobs. We have never been ones for sitting around moping and we thought buying our own business was a real opportunity. But now we've got ourselves in too deep. I don't mind going on myself, but I want Sarah to have the time off she deserves."

Exercise

Where are you now and what are your issues?

Your own age and life-stage probably falls broadly into one of the categories we've outlined above. Look at the following checklists. Pick your relevant life-stage (or two if you feel your situation is transitional or comprises more issues) and tick off where you stand on the issues; then add some issues of your own. It's useful to make a quick assessment of your position. Obviously, the more you can clock up in the 'Under control' column, the better you're doing in staying on top of your changing issues.

In your Balance Book, write more details about the top three or more issues for which you have ticked 'On the horizon' or 'Action required'. Put down on paper the likely timings of those events which are looming, and what effect they will have on your life when they do occur. For those which are already affecting you, write a list of the possible actions you could take in the near future and rank them in the order of most feasible and most likely to attain a satisfactory outcome.

Share these with your partner, with someone else who will be affected by the changes or with a close friend or colleague. Make a note of their responses, especially if they express viewpoints which had not occurred to you. If the issues arising affect other people – such as children's education or the care of elderly relatives – ask their opinions and write down their positions before making decisions on future plans.

Starting out

WORK	Under control	Action required	On the horizon
Decisions about what type of work you want			
Getting the right qualifications/experience			
Finding a job			
Learning the ropes/fitting in at work			
Managing your workload			
Organizing travel/commuting			
Assessing options for moving up/moving on			
Improving your terms and conditions			
Accessing workplace benefits, eg training, wider experience			
Planning a longer-term career path			
Other issues:			

HOME	Under control	Action required	On the horizon
Budgeting for/living within your income			
Finding the right accommodation at the right price			
Negotiating ground rules with flatmates/parents			
Starting/maintaining partner relationships			
Organizing domestic life: shopping, cooking, cleaning, washing, ironing …			
Maintaining your social life, friends and family relationships			
Staying healthy – eating the right food, exercising, relaxing			
Saving enough for planned expenditure, eg a PC, holidays and future plans			
Taking professional advice on savings/pensions			
Other issues:			

Settling down

WORK	Under control	Action required	On the horizon
Maintaining/adjusting your career plan			
Continuing to gain appropriate qualifications/ experience			
Managing your workload effectively			
Sustaining good workplace relationships			
Assessing options for moving up/moving on			
Improving your terms and conditions			
Accessing workplace benefits, eg training, wider experience, financial options			
Familiarization with employer policies on flexible working arrangements, breaks etc for future plans, eg starting a family, travel or study plans			
Staying vigilant about workplace changes, possible redundancy, closure of company			
Other issues:			

HOME	Under control	Action required	On the horizon
Budgeting for/living within current and projected income			
Revising accommodation needs: understanding legal, financial, maintenance, insurance etc aspects of ownership			
Negotiating ground rules of long-term relationships			
Managing domestic life. shopping, cooking, cleaning, washing, ironing …			
Maintaining social life, friends and family relationships			
Staying healthy – eating the right food, exercising, relaxing			
Managing savings for short-term major expenditure, eg a car, holidays, home furnishing and equipment			
Putting long-term savings/pensions, life assurance schemes, a will into place			
Other issues:			

Young families

WORK	Under control	Action required	On the horizon
Adjusting your career plan to current circumstances			
Managing your time and workload effectively			
Sustaining good workplace relationships, communications with managers, colleagues, clients and HR			
Staying up to date with employer policies on flexible working arrangements, breaks etc as childcare/education circumstances change			
Accessing workplace benefits, eg subsidized/on-site childcare, free information, helplines, financial options			
Staying up to date with your area of work			
Remaining vigilant about workplace changes, possible redundancy, closure of company			
Maintaining an open mind about making career changes that will suit your current and planned lifestyle			
Other issues:			
HOME	**Under control**	**Action required**	**On the horizon**
Budgeting for/living within current and projected income			
Revising accommodation needs, if necessary			
Negotiating ground rules of shared parental responsibilities			
Giving children quality time			
Finding appropriate childcare – needs change with different ages and stages			
Maintaining social life, friends and family relationships			
Staying healthy – eating well, exercising, relaxing			
Consider outside help, for example cleaning, gardening			
Update long-term savings/pensions, life assurance schemes, wills			
Other issues:			

The sandwich years

WORK	Under control	Action required	On the horizon
Revisiting career plans – are they still appropriate to current or looming circumstances?			
Renegotiating working options – hours and place of work			
Managing your time and workload effectively			
Assessing options for moving up/moving on			
Staying up to date with your area of work, technological changes			
Start assessing learning/experiential requirements of a new area of work			
Consider 'privatizing' your expertise in self-employment or consultancy role			
Remaining vigilant about workplace changes, possible redundancy, closure of company			
Other issues:			
HOME	**Under control**	**Action required**	**On the horizon**
Budgeting for/living within your income			
Renegotiating house rules with partners/children			
Equalizing distribution of domestic chores: shopping, cooking, cleaning, washing, ironing …			
Preparing for likely eldercare situations			
Personal time and time with partner			
Maintaining your social life, friends and family relationships			
Staying healthy – eating the right food, exercising, relaxing			
Maintaining healthy partner relationships: communicate, compromise, enjoy single and couple breaks, holidays and activities			
Contribute maximum possible to long-term savings/ pensions, life assurance schemes. Update wills			
Other issues:			

Moving on

WORK	Under control	Action required	On the horizon
Revisiting career plans – are your needs and interests still in line with your earlier ideas?			
Renegotiating working options – days, hours and place of work			
Managing your time and workload effectively and to your best advantage			
Assessing options for changing type or nature of work – eg secondment, volunteering or community-based work			
Staying up to date with your area of work, technological changes etc during breaks			
Considering 'privatizing' your expertise in self-employment or consultancy role			
Remaining vigilant about workplace changes, possible redundancy, closure of company			
Other issues:			
HOME	Under control	Action required	On the horizon
Budgeting for/living within your (possibly lower) income			
Prioritizing time for active pursuits, travel etc to avoid later regrets			
Considering downsizing accommodation requirements			
Preparing for likely health issues, for self, partners or others			
Maintaining your social life, friends and family relationships			
Staying healthy – eating the right food, exercising, relaxing			
Maintaining healthy partner relationships: communicate, compromise, enjoy single and couple breaks, holidays etc			
Contribute maximum possible to long-term savings/pensions, life assurance schemes. Update wills			
Other issues:			

CHAPTER 2

This is your work-life

Identity, work and home

If someone you've just met for the first time asks you "What do you do?" what is your response? Do you tell them what you do at home – "I run a house and work on my garden"? Or do you tell them what you do with your leisure time – "I go to the gym a couple of times a week, play tennis occasionally and go to the theatre regularly with friends"?

You might respond in either of those ways, or a number of others, but you'll probably respond to this question with some information about your work. You might make it vague and mention the market sector you work in ("I'm in publishing") or you might be quite specific about your role – "I'm a small business advisor". Either way, you are likely to use a statement of this kind to establish the primary elements of your identity with a new contact.

If you've ever been out of work when someone asks you this question you'll know the kind of discomfort, even depersonalization, that not being able to describe your work identity can cause. You may have opted to take a break from your current job to make a move in a new direction, or have been laid off at work. People with caring responsibilities, such as women who have given up paid employment to care for young children, find themselves in this position. Carers often feel they have become invisible to those immersed in the world of work.

Karen

> "I used to meet up with work colleagues after I stopped work to become a full-time mum. After a while it seemed like people assumed I'd have nothing to say about anything other than nappies and playgroups. In the end I got fed up with trying to join in with the gossip and looking at people's patronizing expressions when I told them how the baby was doing."

Admitting to being unemployed can also cause embarrassment, with the assumptions of failure that others (and perhaps you) can make. It's easier if you can define yourself by your profession, whether you are working or not; actors, with their unreliable employment patterns, traditionally deflect such embarrassment by saying they're 'resting' when they are between roles, and rely on the perceived glamour of their profession to maintain their outward identity. In other lines of work it can prove much harder to maintain a sense of self if your working life is either non-existent, or somehow incompatible with how you'd like to see yourself, or be seen by others.

If your work is what you present to others as the first symbol of your identity, remember that your home life is an equally important, if less up-front, factor in your self-perception, and the way you want others to see you. Your relationships, your role within your family and your home environment are all building blocks around which you construct your identity. Changes in these, whether positive (such as becoming a parent or up-grading to a new home) or negative (such as losing a partner, breaking social contacts or moving to a less desirable area) affect how you feel about yourself and how you think others see you.

If you want to develop a good sense of balance between your work and home life, it's worthwhile exploring which aspects of work and home you use to define yourself, how well these fit together and whether as a combination or individually they are providing you with the personal identity you really want for yourself.

Work and identity

Before the Industrial Revolution, for generation after generation, our ancestors were born into the working lives they were destined to follow. While some men, and a few women, went off to 'seek their fortunes' or to find a better way of subsisting, the majority of people followed their parents' footsteps and provided skills or labour suited to the needs of their community. In the English language, traditional family names reflect three types of identity: an area of work or skills (Smith, Farmer, Archer, Mason); the community or environment in

which you lived (Green, Hill, London, Scott); or personal attributes
(Good, Redhead, Little, Savage). Even amongst the wealthier classes,
careers were often allocated on the basis of family order, so first sons
might go into the legal or medical professions, middle sons into the
armed forces and younger sons into the church. Work identities for
upper class women were almost always negative as they were only
required to work due to poverty and/or failure to find a husband.

The way you talk about your work is a strong indicator of the way
you've built your work into your identity. If you say "I am a teacher/
priest/doctor/pianist/miner" you probably see your work as a vocation
and use your skills or craft as a way of defining the kind of person you
are. The above examples are a way of presenting yourself as a 'giver of
wisdom and knowledge', 'spiritual person of God', 'healer and scien-
tist', 'creative artist' and 'hard-working member of a traditional
community'. You may be someone who identifies strongly with the
way of life your job represents, and who uses an active way to describe
your employment, such as "I drive a truck", "I sell insurance", "I coach
swimmers", "I represent writers". Or you may be one of the diminishing
number of employees who identify themselves strongly with the image
and/or community of their employer, and use this to define themselves, such as "I work for Citibank", "I'm a Qantas air steward", or "I'm
an aid worker for the Red Cross".

Today, in theory at least, we have much more choice about the kind
of work we do. Your choices, though, will be influenced (positively or
negatively) by your parents' choices and attitudes; your innate and
perceived abilities; your ambition and the way it was nurtured at
home, at school and in the community where you grew up; your
education; your financial requirements and aspirations; your ethical
and personal values, and the element of chance.

Exercise

Why do you feel the way you do about your work?

If you feel it might be useful to unravel some of the background to your work choices to date, briefly complete the following sentences.

My father's job made me feel: (eg proud, special, embarrassed)	....
My mother's job made me feel: (eg secure, intimidated)	....
My school/teachers made me feel I was: (eg clever, a plodder, unsuccessful)	....
Among my peer group I have always seen myself as: (eg a high flyer, dumb, the joker)	....
I thought I would be good at my first job because: (eg it was what I wanted to do, it seemed easy, I never thought I'd be bad at it)	....
I've always seen work as a way to make enough money to: (eg pay the basics, impress my friends, become a millionaire)	....
My choices of work have reflected my belief in: (eg public service, market forces, personal service is what counts)	....
I've been lucky/unlucky with my work because: (eg the jobs I want come my way/I'm no good at interviews)	....

Whatever you have written or just thought about, these perceptions made up a large part of the identity you took from your childhood into the workplace. They have contributed to the reasons you went into your first job, why you have followed your particular career path and who and what you perceive yourself to be as a working person. Look at the work experience and skills you have accumulated to date – are these still appropriate beliefs to hold about yourself, or is it time to move on from these early attitudes?

In your Balance Book write more about any of these areas which you feel strongly about. In relation to each, ask yourself the question *why* and write as much as you can in response. Where you have written something negative about yourself in the exercise, for example about how your teachers or peer group made you feel about yourself, write something positive about how they should have made you feel.

Rob

Rob was surprised to find what the exercise showed him about his own attitude to work. He said he was embarrassed about his father's pride in working for the bank, and slightly ashamed of his intelligent mother working as a receptionist. "At school I was always compared badly to my big sister, who seemed to be good at everything, while I was bad at every-thing except sport. I guess being good at sport was cool and I talked it up by saying I was going to go professional." Rob realized that he had never thought about work in terms of a career, only about earning some money in the short term. "I assumed I'd succeed in my first job because you've got to be really stupid not to be able to stack shelves in a supermarket. What I didn't understand was that it would be really hard work and totally boring, so in the end I turned out to be bad at it as well and they fired me. I suppose believing a career would turn me into someone like dad hasn't been a very positive influence. I could try and think along more positive lines".

Jonathan

Jonathan, on the other hand, was almost amused by the clear path to his choice of work. His father was a teacher and his mother a midwife, and although he was an average student at school, his teachers appreciated his hard work. As an only child he was a bit of a loner and saw himself as 'different' among his peer group. "I thought I'd be good at nursing because I was told I was a kind and caring boy, and I think I chose geriatrics because I enjoyed spending time with older people like my parents – they were less threatening than people my own age. I never wanted money for its own sake, so I always saw work as providing just a comfortable lifestyle, and that fits with my belief in public service and personal dignity." Jonathan sees himself as lucky because there will always be a demand for his skills – "and also I'm confident that I'm good at what I do."

Your investment in work

However long or short your work history, you will have made emotional, financial and social investments in your job or career. Your feelings of self-worth are largely tied up with your job – how well you do it, how much your contribution is appreciated, how reliant your employer is on your skills and experience. You've contracted to work for the salary your employer pays and this is probably the most concrete way you value your work, and therefore yourself. Your job may also provide you with a pension and various types of other financial and 'in kind' benefits – from health insurance to childcare. You may also have made other financial investments in your work, from moving house to be close to your workplace to maintaining an appropriate work wardrobe or paying for training or equipment to improve your skills and performance.

The social element of your work is probably as important to you as your personal and financial investments. Your colleagues form a major social network, whether you see them as friends outside the workplace or not, and a surprising number of people meet lovers and life partners through work. The building in which you work may offer places to meet, eat and chat, as well as other social media like phones, faxes and e-mail facilities. Everyone has a social role at work, as well as a job function, and teams often behave like families, with parent figures, more vulnerable members, a joker and so on. The longer you work in any one job, the deeper your investments and the harder it can be to move on, even when it is clearly in your interest to do so.

Work affects your identity in other settings as well. Your job brings you status, self-respect and the respect of others. The desire to do well at work motivates you to achieve and provides (in some cases dictates) your daily routine and an overall structure for your life. You may view work as a vocation, or simply find it endlessly inter-esting, in which case work, to a large extent, is your life. In such cases your values and/or your talents will have informed your choice of work and that work will form a major part of your identity. At the other end of the spectrum, some of you will gain your identity from a belief, skill, involvement or talent from which you can't earn money, such as a sport or art form, a hobby or interest, spiritual beliefs, community activity or your family role. If you're in this posi-tion you may see work as little more than a means of funding that activity, and yet that too can give you a strong investment in your paid employment.

Exercise

What dividends are you earning on your work investments?

Fill in the following checklists (tick the appropriate boxes) to see where you are reaping the greatest rewards from your present job.

EMOTIONAL REWARDS	Good	Average	Poor
The sense of personal reward I get from my work is:			
The value my manager(s) place(s) on my contribution is:			
The value my colleagues place on my contribution is:			
The feedback I get from my customers/clients is:			
My feeling of involvement in what my organization/ profession achieves through its work is:			
Telling people what I do for a living makes me feel:			
My friends/family think that the work I do is:			
TOTAL:			

FINANCIAL REWARDS	Good	Average	Poor
I consider that for the work I perform my pay is:			
The other financial benefits that I receive from my job (eg pension, insurance, childcare subsidy) are:			
The non-financial benefits I receive as part of my work (such as gym membership, subsidized meals) are:			
My working conditions, such as sick leave/pay, maternity, paternity, parental, study leave/pay are:			
In my work I am able to access professional training and personal development, which I consider to be:			
The return on the investments I have made in living near or travelling to my workplace are:			
What I earn from my job allows me to fund my lifestyle and interests in a way which I consider:			
TOTAL:			

SOCIAL REWARDS	Good	Average	Poor
My work colleagues are:			
The opportunities to make friends through work are:			
The chance of meeting a lover/partner at work is:			
The social side of work (lunches, gossip, drinks) is:			
The social areas (café, rest rooms) in my workplace are:			
My family's participation in work social events is:			
The status and respect I receive from doing my job are:			
TOTAL:			

Which area of rewards had the highest total of 'Good' ticks? Which had the highest total of 'Poor' ticks? Which column overall did you score highest in?

When you've counted up your ticks for your total scores and worked out in which area (emotional, financial, social) your work investments are paying the highest dividends (and whether your overall return from your work situation is Good, Average or Poor), write down the heading of your highest totalling area. Then, in your Balance Book, write as much as you like in answer to these three questions:

1 Why do I find this area the most rewarding in my work?

2 Do I feel that this is the most valuable aspect of my work?

3 What can I do to make my investment in this area return an even higher dividend?

Take the middle totalling area. Write as much as you like in answer to these three questions:

1 Is this aspect of my work of secondary importance?

2 If it is, am I happy with that? If not, how can I make my investment return a higher dividend?

3 Is it the nature of the job that makes this area less attractive to me?

Finally, take the lowest totalling area. Write as much as you like in answer to these three questions:

1 Why is this aspect of my work the least satisfactory to me?

2 What can I do to improve the return on my investment in this area?

3 What is this low score telling me about my job?

Now look at your combined totals. If you scored highest in the 'Average' or 'Poor' columns, write some answers to these questions:

1 How do I feel, knowing that most of what I have invested in my work is only returning average or poor rewards?

2 What does that say about my work?

3 What can I do to improve the return on my investment in my work?

Anthony

Anthony was struck by the fact that only the financial rewards of his work now looked 'good' to him. The only emotional reward that he scored above average was 'Telling people what I do for a living makes me feel good' and the only great social reward from his job was status and respect. "The trouble is, feeling that I can't do my job properly any more means that even status and respect aren't real. I can get respect from other people about my job title and working for the bank, but I know it doesn't mean anything any more. And the more I think about how well I'm getting paid, the more scared I am of losing my job." The emotional and social aspects of Anthony's work used to be at least as important as the money, and the loss of these was upsetting him: "In the old days things seemed much more straightforward, customers respected you and you knew the bank was looking after you."

Anthony saw, perhaps for the first time, that having invested his commitment in the bank he had some responsibility to get a return on it. He said he would have to face up to the fact that the world has changed, and that it was down to him to find a way of adjusting to it. "I have invested a lot in my job, emotionally and socially, and I don't want to lose on that investment, any more than I want to lose the salary. I won't get the old way of life back, but if I could just get on top of the work once more I'd gain customers' respect again and hopefully my managers' and colleagues' too."

Lisa

Lisa didn't think she had been in her job long enough to have made much investment in it, but she realized that she had a big emotional investment in wanting to work in the media. "I have thought about ways I could get more return on my investment. This is my list of ideas: I could do some training in a more specific area, such as film and television finance, or set design and construction – I quite like the idea of both of those; I could apply for other jobs, everybody 'job hops' in this industry and it can look good on your CV to have moved around; or, and this looks like the easiest option – but I might find it the most difficult – I could be more pushy about doing what I want here. When you look at what you actually need to be getting out of a job, it makes you think about how to achieve it."

Home and identity

Of course, the life you lead outside work contains many elements that you use to build your personal identity, even though they are not necessarily the first things you would mention to define yourself to a new contact. After your work identity, the next disclosure you are likely to make is whether you are single or partnered. The clearer cut, traditional positions of being single or married are the easiest to add to the identikit description you're presenting, and around which easy and acceptable social assumptions can be formed. Being separated, divorced or widowed, though, may carry implications that either you, or other people, may feel uncomfortable with. There are no equivalent single words with which you can communicate that you are with a long- or mid-term partner, just starting a new relationship, with a second or third long-term partner, or have more than one relationship. If you find it hard to communicate your identity clearly to others it may be that you personally feel uncomfortable with the circumstances of your working life and/or your personal life and how well or badly they reflect your ideal identity.

Conversations around identity often follow a typical pattern: after work, whether or not you are in a long-term partner relationship is likely to surface. If you are single, you will probably move on to talk about your leisure or sport activities (football, music, holidays, fashion); if you are part of a couple without offspring, this is when you are most likely to introduce facts about your partner (particularly their work identity) and your domestic situation (cars, house prices and location). If, on the other hand, you have children, your status as a parent is what you are most likely to present as the next most significant factor in your external identity, with issues like childcare, school, your children's positive attributes and common, minor problems of parenthood all contributing to your social persona.

More deeply embedded, though less overtly communicated to new contacts, are what you have carried into your current identity from your family of origin, including race, nationality, how and where you grew up. The journey you have taken from your culture of birth to the culture you have developed in your individual or family life, with its spiritual and ethical beliefs, community relationships and friends you have surrounded yourself with, are all materials from which you construct your internal identity.

Exercise

What is your identity outside work?

Write a phrase to describe yourself against the areas which are significant to you. For example, if you have unusual parents, children or interests, these may figure prominently as part of your identity. Alternatively, if you are a man, of a majority ethnic group, or heterosexual, these aspects of your identity may not seem worth noting.

Gender	....
Ethnicity/nationality	....
Age/life-stage	....
Sexual orientation	....
Education	....
Religion	....

Appearance	....
Personality	....
Socio-economic background	....
Current socio-economic status	....
Family of origin, special qualities	....
Home	....
Cars	....
Partner/marital status	....
Parental status	....
Social life/friends	....
Extended family	....
Skills/abilities	....
Interests/hobbies	....

Does the above summarize the tangible facts of your own internal identity and/or the identity you like to present to the outside world? If not, write down in your Balance Book what you feel is missing. Are there differences between how you see yourself and how you would like others to see you? Describe what it is about yourself that you would not like others to be aware of.

Take the three areas which you think are most fundamental to your identity and write some more about them.

Naomi and Ed

> Naomi was surprised to see that Ed's top three identity points were his relationship with her, being a 'potential parent' and planning to have a home office. She said that was not the identity he presented to his friends or his colleagues – or even to her. "I would have said his big three were more about the IT industry, having a good lifestyle and then perhaps home and car jointly, or maybe his soccer team. It's been quite revealing and I see I have to take his plans for a new business much more seriously."

> Ed thought Naomi had come up with a few surprises herself. "Naomi doesn't usually make much of her African roots, and she's certainly not a practising Muslim."

> Perhaps because her mother was ill and they were thinking about children, these aspects of Naomi's identity seemed more important at the moment. "All the culture, the history, the relationships that I grew up with are still in my head, even if I don't talk about them. While they haven't had much bearing on my life here, up to now, they will do if I have a child. And perhaps my mother being ill makes me feel I have some more responsibility to my culture…"

> This exercise had shown both Ed and Naomi some things they didn't know about each other and what they wanted to happen when they had a child.

They said they would have to talk through a lot of issues about careers and childcare and find the right balance for them both.

Balancing work and home identities

Your own internal sense of identity is fundamental to the feeling of balance you are able to achieve in your life. If you have a 'work' identity which is incompatible with aspects of your 'home' identity, or *vice versa*, it won't be easy to create a comfortable sense of balance between the two areas of your life. For example, if you see yourself at work as a manager who is able to control your team and delegate work you consider less interesting, and at home have a partner who is happy to run the domestic side of your life which you consider tedious, you will probably find your work and home identities are satisfactorily congruent. However, if you have the same work situation, but your partner also has a responsible and demanding job and expects you to share the domestic chores, you may find yourself having difficulty reconciling the two identities.

Transitions in one or both areas of your life will usually involve redefinitions of identity. At work, a new job, promotion, redundancy or a team reorganization can all require you to re-evaluate how you view yourself, and how others see you. These sorts of changes will also impact on your home life and may lead to a renegotiation of identity between yourself and your partner, family and friends. Equally, major life changes such as leaving home, becoming a parent, moving house or location, even upgrading your car, can prompt changes in your identity, and sometimes a change in one aspect will have to be matched by a conscious change in another. For example, if, as an ambitious executive, you become a parent for the first time, you may have to reconcile an identity based predominantly in your work with that of a committed parent wanting to spend more time at home and espousing 'softer' personal values. This may take time and involve a cognitive process to bring about a comfortable balance.

Gillian, finding what really mattered to her

"I had an exciting media career before the kids were born and I thought I would go back to it as soon as I could. But when I was ready to go back to work I found it was really hard to go on moving up the career ladder and spend the time I wanted to at home. Eventually the stress of trying to combine being a high-flying TV producer and a 'good enough' mother forced me to consider how I really wanted to see myself. Looking after my children at least some of the time was non-negotiable, so I had to make some decisions about what was really important to me on the work side. I realized that I could do without the amount of money I'd been earning, and I could do without the status – but what really mattered was to see myself as 'creative'.

"So I analyzed the areas of my work that gave me the most satisfaction – and really contributed to my sense of personal identity – and thought about what I would like to do and was not able to do as a producer. I decided to resign from my job, but negotiated myself some pieces of free-lance work to get myself started. I kept up my contacts and gradually I re-invented myself as a writer and script editor. The first 18 months were hard in a number of ways: I had less money; people thought I'd been sacked or had just disappeared and the work came in sporadically. Sometimes I had none and sometimes more than I could cope with – it was feast or famine. But I felt I was doing the right thing by my children, and as I achieved a more even flow of work, and developed my skills, I settled down very comfortably with my new identity as a writer.

"Now, even though the children are older, I can't imagine going back into an office situation, with long hours and all the hassle. I have more self-respect for the work I do and I can be more objective about whether I want to take on certain projects or work with certain people. And that's all to do with knowing who you are and what really matters to you."

Your ability to maintain a good balance between your work and home identities is also affected by the increasingly rapid changes in the workplace. You are far less likely than previous generations to stay in one job, or even a single profession, for the whole of your working life, and thus your work identity may undergo radical shifts in quite short periods of time. If this involves being without work for any length of time, or if you are uncertain about how long your current employment will last, the robustness of your identity may suffer; it will be important to be able to adjust your sense of personal identity to a more fundamental level.

For example, as a man you may believe that one of the most important functions of your work is to provide financially for your family. If you are unable to do this for any reason, the balance between your work and home identities will suffer. Equally, as a woman you may retain within your 'home' identity the belief that a good mother spends a certain amount of time at home with her children. If the interest of your job, or financial necessity, requires you to work full-time or long hours you may feel that you are compromising your identity as a good mother. In such cases, it is helpful to take time to examine the assumptions that underlie your work and home identities and how – if you are to achieve a comfortable balance – you can redefine those identities to fit more advantageously together.

Oliver, finding balance as a student

"When you first go away to college your top priority is to get out and meet people, make friends and have a good time. For most people it's the first time they've lived away from home and it can be hard to organize yourself, even things like doing your own washing and not spending too much money. Also, you have to get used to a whole different way of working – there's no daily routine of lessons like at school and you have to find your own way of getting the work done, going to libraries, finding materials. I was living in college accommodation my first year so didn't have to cook or shop much, and to be honest there wasn't much pressure about work. But in my second year I moved into a house with a group of friends and then there was a whole new balance to be worked out domestically, and a much greater pressure of work and exams.

"Now I'm in my third year, and I think I've found a pretty good balance between work, life in the house and having a good time. It's true that as a student you have a lot of time to sit around arguing and discussing things, so I know much more now about who I am and what I care about than when I arrived here. I've also got to start looking for a job for when I finish my degree and, although I don't know exactly what it will be, I know that I'll be looking for something that fits in with my values and philosophy of life, that I enjoy and am interested in doing. I expect to have to work hard, but I won't be looking for something that pays loads of money for really long hours and doesn't give me time for a life outside work."

Exercise

Fits and misfits between your work and home identities

Briefly describe yourself in terms of your *work* identity under the following areas. Then do the same with how you see yourself at home.

	WORK	HOME
Personal style (eg empathetic, motivated, genuine, high achiever, avoids responsibility)		
Relationships (eg egalitarian, defined roles, trusting, nurturing, dependent, one to one)		
Your role (eg breadwinner, carer, hard worker, dutiful son, reliable friend, life and soul of the party)		
Underlying beliefs (eg in hard work, good parenting, what goes around comes around)		
Preferred conditions (eg stability, good planning, spontaneity, frequent change, busy social life)		

Now compare the two columns and check how compatible the identities you have constructed for work and home are. If you find areas where they seem at odds with one another – for example, if you say that at work your personal style is independent and high achieving, but at home you are passive and avoid responsibility – you might want to examine this further and plan to bring some of the qualities you display in one arena into play in the other part of your life. Equally, if at home your preferred conditions are spontaneity and a busy social life, but at work you like stability and good planning, perhaps you are only achieving one of these at the expense of the other. You may find it useful to work on bringing the two identities more in line.

Check the columns vertically, too, for incompatibilities: perhaps you would like to project the personal style of gregarious party animal, but see that your relationships work best on a one-to-one, nurturing level. Or perhaps you maintain a deep-seated belief in the value of hard work in your job, but avoid responsibility for domestic chores. You may like to consider whether one aspect of your work or home identity is compromising or incompatible with others. If so, it may be causing you, or those around you, difficulties which you will need to address.

Dave

> Dave could see that one reason he found it hard to be the husband and father Karen wanted him to be was that he had to be a very different person at work. At work he was used to supervising his team within fixed guidelines without much flexibility in the shift patterns or even around meal breaks and the way leave was booked. "I'm the supervisor and my word goes, apart from the odd bit of discussion. But then when I have my four 'off' days at home between shifts, it's like I'm an intruder." Dave felt uncomfortable with Karen's rigid home routine. Although he recognized its benefits for the children, he felt it inhibited his ability to relax and have fun with them.

Karen

> Karen, on the other hand, said she used to be a different person at work, and it was someone she liked being – efficient, respected and good at

helping other people to enjoy themselves. "I don't have the chance to be that person any more. Maybe I've tried to make our home too regimented, maybe I'm trying to be too much of a 'professional' parent, the perfect mum." She found it hard with Dave on shifts; alone when he was 'on' and aware that he needed to rest when he was 'off', but also wanting more help when he was around. "I can see now that if we're going to get things sorted out we need to work through this identity business, and I've got to let him have his own position more at home. But he's got to see that he can't just come in after four days and expect to be waited on, thinking he's my supervisor, because he's not."

The balance model

Hopefully, the discussion and exercises above have raised some issues about the way you construct your work and home identities, and how you need to bring the two into alignment as a first step towards bringing balance to your life. Writing, or even just thinking, about the assumptions you project into your life (which often lie unchallenged in your subconscious), is a powerful way of clearing the ground to make positive changes. Otherwise you can make practical adjustments but find that they are undermined by your inability to maintain or believe in them.

To have a balanced lifestyle you need to feel a degree of control over your responses to the events, people and organizations with whom you interact. Many factors are outside your direct influence, but the more you feel empowered to adjust circumstances to your best interests, the greater sense of balance you will achieve. To take control, then, you need a structured method of assessing the balance of your life, of determining what you need to change, and in what order. You have to understand what has stopped you achieving better balance so far, how to overcome these barriers and realize what could help you to become a more balanced person. Finally, you need an action plan which will inspire you to achieve the improvements.

The 'Balance Model' is a process which involves all these stages. You can work through it at your own speed, either on a regular basis or in response to particular issues in your life. The steps include:

Balance Check

Aims

Lifeline Objective

Assessing your Aims

Negatives – and overcoming them

Commitments – carrots and sticks

Enacting your Aims

1   The first step is to undertake a 'Balance Check', examining how your life is divided up at the moment, and then devising an ideal breakdown of your time.

2   Taking the differences between your present life structure and how you would like it to be, you will develop some initial Aims to move you from the first position to the second. These are short term, specific, measurable and realistic.

3   From these Aims, and the Balance Check, you can develop a 'Lifeline Objective', which is one (or more) longer-term aspiration describing the overall balance you would like to achieve. Like everything to do with balance, the Aims need constant revision and the Lifeline may stay the same for years, or need updating every year or couple of years.

4 The next step is to Assess the relative importance of your Aims against seven simple parameters and select the most useful to start working on.

5 You will then look at the Negatives, or barriers, to achieving these Aims and how to overcome them.

6 An exercise to develop your Commitment to achieving your Aims results in a clear vision of the benefits of accomplishing them ('Carrot Commitments') and the harm that would result from failing to realize them ('Stick Commitments').

7 Finally, Enacting your Aims: defining the steps you will take towards making the Aims happen, reviewing the support available and finding a 'Balance Partner' to work with.

The first exercise in the Balance Model follows; the rest are spread through Chapters 3, 4 and 5. If you want to go through the Balance Model exercises as a single activity, the page numbers for the seven exercises are given on the Contents page.

Exercise

Balance check 1 – what does your life look like now?

The circle overleaf is a 'Balance Wheel'. Either here, or by drawing your own wheel in your Balance Book, divide the circle into segments representing the amount of time, in an average week, you spend on the most important categories of your life. We have offered some examples, but you may have other aspects to your life, or categorize your activities or interests in different ways. Try to restrict your categories to six areas or less. Do include your versions of the main four headings, even if some of the segments are tiny. Don't spend time calculating the exact amount of hours per week you spend doing housework or driving the car, but respond quickly to how it *feels* to you.

Balance wheel

Self:	**Home:**	**Work:**	**Community:**
Health/fitness	Domestic chores	Time at work	Friends
Relaxation	Admin	Training & devt	Partner
Learning	Maintenance	Core work	Children
Hobbies	DIY	Work at home	Eldercare
Spiritual	Gardening	Admin	Pets
Sport		Commuting	Extended family
Social life			Voluntary work
Travel			Travel

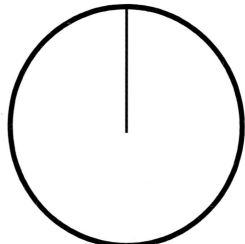

Balance check 2 – what would you like your life to look like?

How does your first Balance Wheel look? If you're like most people, some of the segments will be far bigger than you would like them and others far too small for comfort. Now take a fresh Balance Wheel and repeat the process for how you would *like* the segments to look. Work on reasonable assumptions – such as that you will have to continue to earn a certain amount, you can't spend money you haven't got, wish away inconvenient circumstances or compromise the lives of those around you at work or at home.

Balance wheel

Self:	**Home:**	**Work:**	**Community:**
Health/fitness	Domestic chores	Time at work	Friends
Relaxation	Admin	Training & devt	Partner
Learning	Maintenance	Core work	Children
Hobbies	DIY	Work at home	Eldercare
Spiritual	Gardening	Admin	Pets
Sport		Commuting	Extended family
Social life			Voluntary work
Travel			Travel

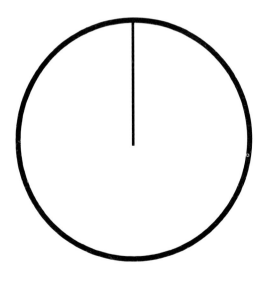

Extended exercise

Look at the differences between your first and second Balance Wheels. In your Balance Book, rank the segments your wheels are divided into in order of their *importance to you*, starting with the most important. Then list the different segments you have divided your two wheels into in *order of size*, starting with the biggest.

Under each heading write about:

- Why you rank its importance as you have.

- Why you devote the time to it that you do.

- Do the size/time and ranking/importance match up on your first Balance Wheel?

- Are they better matched on your second Balance Wheel?

- If not, why is this? (It may be, for example, that you spend far more time on housework than its importance to you warrants because you are a perfectionist; you could make a conscious effort to change this. Or it could be that work is not your highest priority, but takes up the highest proportion of your time because of your financial requirements, which cannot currently be changed.)

Finally, write a few sentences or a paragraph about why you would like to achieve the time distribution represented by your second Balance Wheel and what your life would be like if you could.

Della

Della wanted to be spending less time on the family and the household chores and more time on herself and on work – although she was still not sure what her ideal work would be. "So much of my headspace is taken up by shopping, washing and catering that I hardly seem to have any time to begin looking at what I possibly could do. And yet I'm sure there is something I could get going for myself, whether it's just me as a self-employed person or whether it's starting a small business. But until I make some time to think and do my research, perhaps talk to some other people, nothing's going to happen."

Marie

Marie's second Balance Wheel showed her how much she wanted to reduce the time she spent at work and spend more time on golf and some kind of 'community activity'. The exercise highlighted that she really did want to pursue competitive golf more than her current work hours permitted. "It's also made me realize that I could use my work skills in other ways than at the council. Perhaps some kind of voluntary work might give me more of a sense of purpose, without having to go in for a complete change of direction."

Sarah

Sarah reported that she and Tom had both drawn in a smaller 'Work' segment on their second Balance Wheels, but that she wanted to spend even less time at work time than Tom, and more time with the family. Tom wanted to spend more time taking exercise and getting his health and fitness levels up. He said: "We only live round the corner from the park, and if we got a little dog from an animal shelter I know Sarah would love it and it would give me a reason to go for a good walk every day. But until we can get the work levels down it's not worth even thinking about."

CHAPTER 3

Balanced living – opportunities and threats

THIS CHAPTER COVERS:

● Assessing your material baselines – financial, time, health and well-being, personal development.

● Assessing your emotional baselines – needs, values, tolerations and boundaries.

● Aims and Lifeline Objective(s).

● Assessing your Aims.

● Putting it all together.

The first two chapters of this book have given you the chance to explore the important background influences on your attitudes to your work and personal life. Now it's time to look at the specifics of your current situation. If you want to improve your work-life balance, you'll need to weigh up realistically your basic requirements – those things which you cannot change at present – and then look at the areas where you could make some adjustments. These barriers and opportunities fall into two categories: the material aspects of life, which are perhaps the simplest to evaluate; and the emotional needs we all have, which are as vital to our well-being as food and shelter, but which we often fail to recognize.

Your material baselines

Four areas of your material life provide the cornerstones on which to build balance. These are:

1   Your base-level financial outgoings.

2   The minimum time required for your personal commitments.

3   Your commitment to your health and well-being; and

4   Maintenance of your personal development.

If you haven't clarified your requirements around these four areas they will appear and reappear as barriers to balance in your life.

Your financial requirements

Your ability to provide materially for yourself and your family is dependent to a large extent on the money you earn. Establishing your financial baseline needs are a high priority as you start to think about achieving a well-balanced life, because on the one hand you don't want to limit your options by clinging to short-term status symbols which don't bring the contentment you may crave; and on the other, you don't want to make unrealistic plans for a change in lifestyle which compromise you or your family's ability to meet a basic budget. If you have a partner, your family finances may not be entirely down to you, and achieving better balance for the both of you may require negotiation around your individual working times, your respective rates of pay and division of home responsibilities. Whether you are in a partnership or not, you need to know the facts and figures before you can move on.

Start by answering these fundamental questions. If you don't know the answers off the top of your head go and check your bank statements, credit card statements or cheque book and find them.

• What is the minimum amount you need on a monthly basis to cover the costs of living in your home (including rent or mortgage, related life assurance, building and contents insurance, tax, water, gas, electricity, other maintenance)?

• What is the minimum amount you need to cover consumables (include food and household items, clothes, travel, phones/e-mail/ faxes, post, children's school items, medical costs, leisure activities that you wouldn't wish to forego)?

• Total up your regular contributions to whatever savings schemes you have in place, formally or informally (include pensions, life assurance, savings accounts etc).

• What do any other essential items of expenditure not included above cost you on a monthly basis?

• Add the four totals together to discover your minimum monthly expenditure.

How did these totals make you feel? If there is a comfortable margin between your final total and the monthly household income, you probably didn't get too much of a shock and are in the enviable position of having some room to manoeuvre the balance of your life in relation to your income. For some of you, though, even this sufficiency of money won't feel like good balance, and doesn't recompense you for the stress of, or the dissatisfaction with, your (or your partner's) job.

Marie

> Marie already knew she could easily cover her basic living costs with a reasonable amount left over, but felt it was not enough: "I don't want more money, but I *do* want to feel more fulfilled, more excited by my work and by the rest of my life."

There again, you may have been shocked to find that your household income only just covers (or even does not cover) these outgoings, which don't take into account many things that most of us take for granted like buying desirable but non-essential consumer goods or clothes, going on holiday, spending money on eating or drinking out. It's possible that even though the figures don't add up you still manage to pay for these additional luxuries, but unless you're very laid back about money the effort to maintain a financial balance and perhaps the debts you're running up will be causing you considerable stress.

Karen

> Karen said that although Dave's wages covered their basic living costs they were still paying off the debts for the holiday and the car and that meant they were not making ends meet, despite Dave's overtime. "It's just not worth him working these hours and never seeing the kids for that amount of money and the stress we go through trying to get by."

If you feel your finances are in good balance this is not going to be a major driver for making changes in your life; but there are other material considerations to be taken into account.

Your personal commitments

Quite apart from your current work there are demands on your time which are as important and as immovable as those on your money, and which need to be assessed as rigorously and specifically. Try to calculate the minimum number of hours – on a weekly or monthly basis – you spend on the following, or other, fixed aspects of your life outside work.

- Caring responsibilities (including children – time spent with them and transporting them to school or other carers; dependent adults – long-term sick or infirm partners, parents, relations or friends who depend on your time in person or on the phone, for whatever reason; pets).

- Domestic chores (including household shopping, cleaning, washing, ironing, cooking, tidying).

- Personal/household administration (include paying bills, writing official letters, making necessary phone calls).

So how much time do you spend on the essentials that keep yours and your family's lives running smoothly? Almost all the time that you have outside work? If you're a parent of young children, or one of the sandwich generation, you may find the demands on your time quite stressful and may resent some of the people who make those demands or others who are not sharing this load fairly with you. You may be able to reduce some of your time spent on caring, domestic or administrative tasks if there are others around to negotiate with, but if this is not the case the only adjustment you are likely to be able to make is in the hours or patterns of your work.

Della

When Della added up the hours she spent managing the household, doing things for Anthony and the children, and Anthony's parents, she felt angry: "I've been doing all this for the family all my life and it's time they all grew up and took more responsibility for cleaning, cooking and looking after themselves. My parents-in-law are different, they are getting quite frail; but even so, I can't just be at their beck and call. This is my time and I need to have space for what I want to do."

Conversely, if you are single, or at a moving on stage, you may find yourself in too little demand by others and feel either at a loose end or even guilty at having so much time to yourself. Remember that guilt is really not a useful emotion unless you either translate it into action or dig deeper to see it as a residual part of negative self-esteem. So either get out there and spend time with someone who would really value your company or support, or convince yourself that, yes, it's fine for you to have the luxury of enjoying your favourite pursuits, or spending a day doing nothing for anyone but yourself. If this satisfaction palls then there are plenty of organizations looking for volunteer workers, or there is a wide range of courses (both online and face to face), that would provide an interesting addition to your skills or interests.

The likelihood, though, is that the demands on your finances and time are higher than acceptable to fit your perception of balanced living. They are the areas in which you probably feel you are running up a constant 'debit' balance and which seem to prevent you from developing more balance in your life. On the other side of the equation are a couple of areas in which most of us have an accumulation of 'time credits' which we find ourselves unable to spend. The first of these areas is health and well-being.

Your health and well-being

If you are someone with a consistently heavy workload, particularly if you end up taking work home for the evenings or weekends, or if you work for an organization which encourages you to spend long hours in the office, you are probably neglecting your health and well-being. The same will be true if you are a parent or have eldercare responsibilities (or both), or if you are trying to combine any of the above with additional training or community responsibilities. Assess how many hours maximum, on a weekly or monthly basis, you spend on the following:

- Your physical fitness (include planned exercise of more than 20 minutes duration, such as walking, jogging, swimming, playing sport, aerobics, yoga, working out).

- Planning, shopping for and preparing a varied and healthy diet.

- Your mental or physical relaxation (include meditation, prayer or other spiritual practice, physical relaxation techniques such as auto-suggestion, listening to music, controlled breathing).

- Being alone or with chosen companions, enjoying yourself (include reading for relaxation, shopping for pleasure, treating yourself to something as small as a good cup of coffee – out of the home – visiting an art gallery, theatre, concert, sports event).

Unless your life is already pretty well balanced, you've probably found you don't spend much time on more than one (if that) of the above activities. Most of us are sufficiently short-sighted and stressed out to tell ourselves we don't have time for these sorts of 'self-indulgent' pursuits, when we should know from experience that they are enormously positive and easily repay the time we spend on them.

Tom

Tom said again that he and Sarah were "exhausted" by their cleaning business. It was hard enough for them to keep their house clean and eat properly, let alone relax or take some exercise. "That's what I thought we'd be spending our time on at our age, but whenever we sit down with a paper or to watch some TV I've dozed off in ten minutes."

Keeping physically fit with regular exercise maintains all our systems – from the cardiovascular to the immune – thus reducing the time we lose through illness. The exercise itself also produces endorphins, the brain chemicals that promote positive feelings, creativity and energy, which increase our productivity and our ability to deal with stress. Likewise, a healthy and balanced diet gives us a better energy flow, keeps our weight reasonable, helps our brain and body systems to function efficiently and reduces mood swings and lethargy. The more we fall into poor eating habits, the more barriers we put in the way of achieving balanced living. If you have a cup of coffee and a couple of chocolate biscuits at 3.30pm every day for a week, by the end of that week you'll find yourself craving that snack at exactly that time. But if a habit is easy to form, it's also not so hard to break – or even to replace with a better habit. Change the coffee for a mineral water and the biscuits for some fruit, and within a week you'll be actively looking forward to the new, healthier treat.

Naomi

Naomi made some efforts in this direction since thinking about having a baby, and after a couple of weeks of eating more healthily, eating little and often instead of forgetting to have breakfast or lunch, she found she had more energy and didn't need the endless cups of coffee she used to drink to keep going. "Since I'm feeling this much better I'm almost thinking of joining a gym or an aerobics class – but don't push me, I'm not there yet!"

Even if you do maintain an exercise programme and eat healthily, you probably pay less attention than you should to regular periods of essential mental and physical relaxation. You are probably aware that even a few minutes a day spent meditating, breathing or using your preferred way of clearing your mind, reduces stress in measurable physiological ways – eg lowered blood pressure, heart and breathing rate – and allows your mind to process information and problems at a subconscious and very effective level. Likewise, whatever caring and work responsibilities make claims on your time, regular enforced periods of personal sustenance – from 20 minutes with a coffee and a good book to a holiday without children or dependants – enable you to produce better quality work and provide better care to those who need you rather than unrelieved periods of unconditional giving. Related to your personal health and well-being, and also likely to be a 'credit' balance in your life, is your personal development.

Your personal development

Another potential barrier to your ability to achieve a better balanced life is a failure to keep your skills, knowledge and experience up to date. The best employers offer a wide range of training and personal development courses to employees, and if you are lucky enough to work for such an organization it will be easy to take advantage of such offers. If you are less fortunate in your employer, or are self-employed, you will have to make your own opportunities to up-date your saleable attributes (as a future employer, customers or clients will see them) and so make sure you are a suitable candidate for that promotion, new job or whole career move, when it comes your way.

How many of the following opportunities do you take up in a year?

• Signing up to an in-house training course/workshop in a work-related skill or competence.

• Electing to take a training course/workshop in a work-related skill or competence on your own behalf outside work.

• Taking a course (on line, correspondence or face to face) to develop a personal interest or ability.

• Choosing to have a new experience that will broaden your personal perspective and/or enhance your contribution at work and elsewhere (eg overseas holiday, activity holiday, volunteering experience, community work).

If you have done none or few of these in recent years you are building up your own barriers to balanced living. No matter what field you currently work in (or would like to work in), changes in products, services, personnel, clients, customers, technology and ways of working are inevitable. If you want to keep your options open for job progression or career change you have to regard yourself as the only person responsible for maintaining yourself as a valuable commodity. You need to see all your attributes, competencies and experience as additions to your skillset and appropriate to a constantly changing work marketplace.

Dave

> Dave said he would like to think about a change of work, but thought his lack of qualifications combined with his punishing work schedule to pay off the family's debts meant he couldn't consider any other option: "No, I hadn't thought of asking my boss if there was any training they'd give me time off for. Maybe I'll have a chat with him."

Lowering your barriers to balance

To sum up, the areas where you will find your personal barriers to achieving balance can be divided into 'credit' and 'debit' areas. Most of us will find that we perceive ourselves more or less in debit in terms of money and time, working as long and as hard as we can to cover our financial outgoings, and trying to fit caring, domestic and administrative responsibilities into the resulting time deficit. It's worth spending some time thinking of ways in which you could spend less, and talking to people with whom your could share domestic tasks – both of which could result in much needed credits.

It may be helpful if you can make some savings in your financial and time expenditure, but a realistic assessment of your basic requirements in these areas does provide a baseline on which to build a balanced lifestyle. Costs must be covered and children, dependent adults and pets cared for; and you will feel better for knowing what you consider the essentials – although these may not remain static – and what you will not compromise on.

On the other side of the equation, many of us are preserving self-erected barriers to balanced living by not spending enough time or energy on our own health and well-being, or maintaining our work-based or personal skills and interests. To make constructive changes, you need to feel physically good, have a positive mental outlook and consistent energy levels. You'll find all of these come much more readily with as little as 20 minutes sustained exercise three times a week. The more you put into your health and fitness, the more you'll get out. The same goes for eating well: you will feel better if you cut out excesses of sugar, junk food, snacks, coffee, tea, fizzy drinks and alcohol. Ensuring you take even small, regular times for personal relaxation and 'selfish' enjoyment is not, in fact, selfish. Your physical

and emotional health and well-being are key to your ability to maintain your balanced living, and that of those around you.

Similarly, when you keep your skills and interests up to date and relevant you not only keep your mind active and open you also arm
yourself with valuable personal equipment to stay marketable and
flexible in a changing workplace.

Your emotional baselines

We all have emotional needs as well as material ones, and getting
these met is as fundamental to our sense of balance as satisfying physical needs like food and sleep. Unfortunately, these needs are often
much harder to identify and unsatisfied needs can make themselves
felt by long-term but general feelings of dissatisfaction, unhappiness or
anxiety. Identifying your emotional needs – and whether or how they
are met by your current work/home life – is a necessary step towards
achieving a balanced life. While they are consistently unmet, work life
as well as home life will remain unnecessarily stressful.

Your emotional needs

Your personal needs (as opposed to physical needs such as water, food,
warmth and shelter) are those things you must have in order to
operate at your best. You can get through life reasonably well without
having some of these needs met, but you will have to work harder to
be balanced, happy, rewarded and successful. If you have unmet needs
you are probably spending a good deal of energy trying (consciously or
otherwise) to get them met. You are probably treating the symptoms
or finding temporary relief from them in the mistaken belief that this
'problem' is just the way you are. In this context a need is, by

definition, unmet on a long-term basis. When you find a way of meeting that need the symptoms which define it will cease to exist.

Try the following exercise to define your three most pressing unmet needs.

Exercise

From the following 12 headings select those which strike a chord as an area of need for you. Then list in your Balance Book two or three words under each of your chosen headings which accurately describe how you would like to feel or be. It is important that you are honest about these – and it's surprising how hard this can be. Some words will spring to mind instantly and feel right; others may force themselves into your mind almost against your will and you will resist admitting to them, perhaps because you don't want to feel that emotion or meeting this need seems impossible. Bear in mind, though, that your needs are not 'wants', 'shoulds', 'fantasies' or 'wishes'; a need is something you *must* have in order to be your best.

I must:

- BE ACCEPTED (eg approved, respected, included, indispensable, important, taken seriously).

- BE ACKNOWLEDGED (eg appreciated, valued, complimented, thanked, celebrated, famous, credited).

- BE FREE (eg unlimited, independent, self-reliant, in control, able to change, irresponsible).

- BE LOVED (eg liked, cherished, desired, saved, touched, helped, attended to).

- BE NEEDED (eg useful, craved, please others, affect others, improve others).

- BE RIGHT (eg correct, honest, understood, loyal, moral, upright, satisfy others, prove yourself, obey).

- ACCOMPLISH (eg achieve, fulfil, win, gain, strive for, surpass).

- CONTROL (eg dominate, correct, manage, maintain, restrict, be obeyed, authoritative, strong, influential, powerful).

- HAVE SECURITY (eg have guarantees, promises, commitment, exactness, safety, prosperity, abundance, be taken care of).

- HAVE COMMUNICATION (eg be heard, listened to, make a point, share, gossip, have the last word, not be ignored).

- HAVE ORDER (eg perfection, balance, consistency, unchanging, calm, agreement, quiet, checklists).

- WORK (eg career, vocation, performance, responsibility, be busy, make it happen, task, plan).

Now take your list and reduce it to the three most important personal needs. Do this by asking: "If I had this would I be able to achieve my goals without effort?"; "Which ones, if they were met, would make the others seem less important?"; and "Can I live without this one?" This whole process could take you some time; you may not be able to get down to your three main needs in one session. When you have, however, write them out in large letters. We'll come back to them.

Jonathan

Jonathan identified three main needs: to be included, not to be ignored and to be loved unconditionally. He initially included the need to be shown appreciation, but realized that he was getting enough of that from his patients so it wasn't a real need at the moment. "I don't feel included by my team at work, and sometimes I feel ignored. I'm not getting either of those things from my parents, or the unconditional love they used to give me, since I came out. I realize that not getting these needs met is making me feel upset and angry all the time."

Your personal values

Your values form the basis of how you approach your life. The things you value – and how much you value them – affect your attitudes, behaviour, beliefs and choices. When you are living your life according to your values you feel excited, productive, in control and energized. Values include, for example, creativity, teaching, leadership, contributing to or being in a relationship. Unfortunately, most of us are inhibited in the pursuit of our values by our responsibilities to earn money, care for others, meeting unmet needs or just surviving. Once you have identified your key values, though, it is easier to make the changes in your life which will allow you to follow them and achieve better balance through doing so.

Suzanne, full-time freelance journalist

"I suppose I do think I worked out some 'solutions' – these were essentially practical in nature and I felt that I really had to work out my personal values, vis a vis kids and career particularly, before I could organize my time sensibly."

Exercise

For your personal values, repeat the same process you used to identify your needs. From the following 12 headings select those which resonate as key values for you. Then list in your Balance Book two or three words under each of your chosen headings which accurately describe what you feel is important for you to do or be. Again, be honest and open to the unexpected about these. Some words will spring to mind instantly and feel right, others may seem silly or you may just want to skip over them. But these may be hidden values which you have tried to ignore because they seem impossible, or even too enjoyable.

- ADVENTURE (eg danger, experiment, thrill, quest, change, chance).

- CHANNEL (eg to encourage, influence, teach, stimulate, energize, alter, enlighten).

- LEARN (eg discover, uncover, realize, observe, study, gain knowledge, skill, expertise).

- APPEAR (eg beautiful, strong, elegant, glorious, tasteful, individual, attract).

- CREATE (eg design, invent, conceive, paint, build, be original, imaginative).

- CONTRIBUTE (eg serve, provide, offer, help, strengthen, improve, enable).

- FEEL (eg experience, sense, intuit, glow, sympathize, energy, passion, intensity, peace, contentment).

- PLEASURE (eg fun, sex, entertainment, sports, social, bliss, luxury).

- LEAD (eg guide, inspire, rule, model, encourage, mentor, change).

- RELATE (eg be with, connected, in community, bonded, family, nurture, compassion).

- SPIRITUAL (eg religious, devoted, in touch, aware, accepting, enlightened, honouring, at peace).

- ATTAIN (eg expert, master, pre-eminent, set standards, excellence, outdo, success, wealth).

Once again, take your list and reduce it to the three most important personal values. Do this by asking: "If I had this, would I be energized and fulfilled?"; "Which ones do I really long to achieve?"; and "If I could do/be this would life be a whole lot more enjoyable?" Again, this process could take you some time; you may not be able to get down to your three main values in one session. When you have, though, write them out in large letters.

Gina, taking time to find balance

"Finding the balance in my life has taken a number of years. When I ran my own communications company (1986–1993), employing six people, I worked long hours which actually I loved. I loved the work, too. The only thing that bothered me was that I was always in a hurry and so often rude in shops and whenever I was kept waiting. Couldn't they see I was in a hurry? Impatience was running my life and making me not the nicest person to be with.

"One day I went to a demonstration session of 'Voice Dialogue', a method that addresses the different energies/personalities that live inside us. When they asked someone to come up to the stage everyone else looked at their shoes. I immediately raised my arm. In that demonstration session a part of me came out that was very, very tired of all this running around trying to prove to the world (my parents?) that I existed and that I could function. As I became aware of this part of me I allowed it to be there more often. The rigid, efficient, ambitious part of me could rest at weekends and save energy for the busy work week, while with the other part I read a book or listened to music and generally chilled out.

"The second big influence was the 'Transformation Game', which showed me I am not in this life alone. There are forces outside me that want to help me realize who I am and what I have to offer. This game, which was developed in the Findhorn Foundation in Scotland, has shown me that my life wants to flow a certain way and that I have much less stress if I follow it than when I try to direct it, and that miracles always want to happen but can only materialize when we are not standing in the way. I am not controlling my life so much anymore; I go with the flow. I have trained to become a facilitator of the Transformation Game and love to see others make the discovery that they can ask 'Angels' or other love forces to help them in life – even the 'Angel of Efficiency'!

"On the practical side I have a small notebook lying on my desk where I write down everything I need to do – this keeps me from worrying when I lie in bed that I might forget to ring someone or mail something. And when I've done something I cross if off, which gives me a feeling of satisfaction. Also, I don't beat myself up for not doing enough anymore. I am now 47 and finally I know that I do a lot. If sometimes I have let something slip it's not the end of the world, and people will not cross me out of their address book – I am free. It has taken a lot of work to get here, but now that I am here, it's perfect."

Your tolerations

Negative aspects of life (large and small) that we tolerate either consciously or unconsciously at work and at home sap us of energy and enthusiasm. There may be barriers in the workplace to leading a balanced life which seem beyond our control (although this is a good time to confront them); there may be demands at home which could be handled better, but it's important, too, to look at those which are internal and self-imposed. Identifying your tolerations, taking responsibility for them and looking at ways to deal with them is often a big step towards getting needs met and enabling you to live your values.

Exercise

Under the following headings, list in your Balance Book everything that you are currently tolerating and which is having a negative effect on your life.

AT HOME

- Eg your home – exterior, interior, garden, neighbours.
- Eg your partner – behaviour, habits, attitudes, responsibility.
- Eg your children – behaviour, expectations, responsibilities.
- Eg extended family, friends – behaviour, expectations, attitudes.

AT WORK

- Eg your manager – demands, communication, attitude, feedback.
- Eg your colleagues – demands, communication, attitude, feedback, responsibility.
- Eg your clients – demands, attitude, communication, feedback.
- Eg policies, practices and culture which have negative effects on your life.

- Eg work environment – your working space, equipment, noise levels, poor maintenance, inadequate IT.

YOURSELF

- Eg "I can't …"; "I'm no good at …"; "I don't have what it takes to …"

- "He'll only say No …"; "She'll never stick to …"; "I/we can't afford to …"

- "It's not worth the effort to …"; "I haven't got time to …"; "I don't have the right to …"

It helps to write down your tolerations, so keep adding to this list even if you don't yet know how to resolve the problem – the solution will present itself. What are your three key tolerations? Now look for some critical tolerations – something that, when handled, will resolve several tolerations in one go. For example, if you were to give up smoking and/or convince your partner to quit smoking the results could be: to stop your home smelling unpleasant; to release sufficient funds to pay someone to do the cleaning, thus ending your frustration with an unpleasant home environment, your feeling of being put upon and the disputes about housework. You might also lose that nagging cough and the bronchitis you get every winter.

Lisa

> Lisa said she was tolerating being used as a dog's body at work, along with her own worries that she wasn't good enough to take on more than the low level of responsibility in her current job. She asked herself what the critical toleration was. "If I stop myself feeling unconfident about taking on more, perhaps I'll look and act more capable so they'll think I'm more

useful. And if that doesn't happen, at least I should be able to talk to them about what I want to do and ask for more interesting work ..."

Your boundaries

Related to your tolerations are the emotional boundaries you put up around yourself as protection. If these aren't strong enough to maintain a sufficient personal space between you and other people and their demands you will end up feeling under siege, with too many tolerations. Your personal boundaries define how you relate to other people and situations and, if they are inappropriately set, they can leave you unable to say No to excessive demands on the one hand, or if they are unnecessarily robust, make it difficult for you to engage in teamwork on the other. When your boundaries are properly set you feel able to ask for the reasonable changes that you need, at work or at home, and to assess what is reasonable give and take in your relationships with others.

As you examine and deal with your tolerations, your boundaries will reset themselves automatically, but it is worth looking at the material and emotional requirements you have defined through the exercises in this chapter and drawing some unambiguous boundaries around them.

Boundaries for your material needs:

- You now know the minimum amount of money you (and your family/dependants) can live on each month. For your own sense of security, envisage this figure and draw a mental boundary (and perhaps an actual one by keeping the money in a separate account) around that amount and make sure that no one encroaches into it to pay for unplanned 'necessities', treats or a loan.

- In the same way, you have defined the minimum amount of time per week or month that you need to spend on your personal responsibilities. Now draw a mental line around that time and don't let work commitments or other demands reduce that time to less than you feel comfortable with.

- Try to draw up a practical schedule for maintaining your health and well-being, and don't let other pressures make inroads into your timetable.

- Sign up and prepay for courses, workshops, activities, holidays etc that are part of your personal development plan; these commitments act as useful boundaries.

Boundaries for your emotional needs:

- When you have decided on your three key emotional needs, your next step is to work on strategies to get these needs met – permanently. These must be things for you to do, although they may include asking other people to play a part (for example, to give you more positive feedback, include you more or be more physically affectionate). Define some clear boundaries (either internally or expressed to others) about what kinds of behaviours from others stop you meeting your needs, and which you will no longer tolerate. At first you may need to establish boundaries which are more than you actually need, but there are no justifications for letting anyone behave towards you in ways which hurt, deflect, exploit or control you.

- Having identified your three key values, and understood why they are important to you, you can now go on to decide on actions that will re-orientate your life around these values. These may be major changes, for example to change jobs, remove yourself from a destructive relationship, free yourself from addictions; or less difficult, such as upgrading your wardrobe, recycling your garbage or shelving plans for an expensive consumer item you don't really need. Drawing boundaries around your values will involve demarcating where it is destructive to be drawn into actions and positions which move you away from your values.

Sarah

Sarah thought that she and Tom needed to put up some boundaries between themselves and the business: "When staff say they can't make a shift we just say 'OK, we'll do it'. Perhaps we need to tell people No, we can't always step in, we have other commitments too. If we start saying No we'll have to come up with other solutions, and perhaps other people will take more responsibility if we take less."

Paul, 35, teacher

"I am a teacher at an inner city boys' high school. I used to be 'in Advertising', but that was far too easy, or so I thought. I have been a teacher for nine years, and have enjoyed the feeling of doing something useful and rewarding, rather than the advertising which, although more lucrative, seemed shallow to me. I moved on from being a simple classroom teacher to being a head of year; I was making progress, and loving it. I was putting in the effort and the hours, but I had no family commitments and was able to go out most evenings and relax over a few beers. It seemed I had got the balance right.

"Friends and colleagues told me I looked tired, to slow down and not work so hard. OK, I did sometimes feel pretty exhausted and I was probably spending far too much money, but I still felt good. Then everything started going wrong. I went in to work as usual; the morning was stressful, but in a normal way. By lunchtime, though, I was feeling very strange, distant somehow; and I was getting some chest pains. I carried on as usual for a bit and tried to ignore it, but finally I had to give up and go home (my first sick day in three years). Things didn't improve and at last I went to the doctor who diagnosed stress. I was outraged, and I felt a failure. It took a while for me to come to terms with the fact that I wasn't coping, that the balance was very far from right. In the end, the doctor had to sign me off work for five weeks; nothing could be resolved while I was still coping with the day-to-day stresses of the job. This was very traumatic for me, but in the end it turned out to be a good move. Not only did I have the time physically to unwind, but I began to realize just how tied up I had become with work. Yes, teaching is more than a job, but a line has to be drawn somewhere.

"Since my return I have rearranged my duties; taking less responsibility for discipline and pastoral care, the most demanding parts of my job. I have watched my old deputy rush around madly (just like I used to do). I have rediscovered how to teach rather than just shout, and everyone tells me how well I look. Part of me feels less fulfilled than I did, but I do feel physically better and have more 'mind space' to think about what to do next. I never intended to be a teacher forever; now is my chance to find something rewarding, but less stressful. I am thinking of buying a flat now, so some extra cash wouldn't go amiss either!"

Aims and lifeline objectives

The next steps in the Balance Model will help you to frame your needs, values, tolerations and boundaries in a concrete way so you can move forward. Remember, the A and L of Balance stand for Aims and Lifeline. The first are a set of short-term aims that you will define for yourself, which are steps on the way to achieving your 'Lifeline' – a longer-term objective (or objectives) that encompasses your needs and values. Look again at the two Balance Wheels you completed in Chapter 2. Would a move towards the second, ideal, wheel, with its more balanced division of your life, help you meet your needs and values? If not, perhaps you need to make some more adjustments.

Take some time now to look again at the differences between your two wheels and where you want changes to occur; at the decisions you have made about your material needs; at the three key needs and values you have identified; and at the list of tolerations you have made.

Bearing all these in mind, take some time to carry out the following exercise.

Exercise

Formulate three Aims in the area of your work, and three Aims for your life outside work, which will move you in the right direction of your second balance wheel. These Aims should be specific – for example, not "I want to get fit" but "I will work out twice a week"; not "I'll try and leave the office on time more often" but "I will organize my work so I can leave at 5.30pm three days a week". The Aims should also be measurable, eg "I want to spend an hour with the kids before bedtime each night" rather than "I want to spend more time with my children"; or "I will finish off project X within two weeks". And they must be realistic. Don't write down "I want to buy a Porsche" unless you really will be able to, but rather "I plan to save x,ooo for the deposit on a new car by this time next year."

When you've written your six Aims – or more if you find they come tumbling out onto the page – then it's time to write your Lifelines. These are longer-term, over-arching objectives that cover all your other Aims and take into account your needs and values. For example, "I want to have a job which allows me to contribute to the community and extends my business skills; and I want to be the best parent I can be for my children." Or "I want to be promoted to area manager within the next year and access the leadership training which goes with it. I want to be earning enough within two years to move to a bigger house in a better area."

Try to make all your Aims and Lifelines positive: "I will do …", not "I don't want to …" You might want to try out a few in your Balance Book, but write your final six Aims and Lifeline(s) down on the form opposite.

Ed

> Ed found it easier to write his Lifeline first. He said: "Within two years I will have started my own business which I will structure to give me the flexibility to be the best father and husband I can, whatever that takes". By this he meant that he was going to have to listen to Naomi's views about family life, make some compromises and be more open about his own expectations. His three home Aims were: to make specific time to talk to Naomi about family life; to check out the finances and the practicalities of moving to a house that could be used as a work base; and to spend more time at home. His work Aims were: to talk to colleagues about starting the consultancy; to sign up for a couple of courses at work; and to start organizing work more efficiently, as if already self-employed. "Thinking those Aims and Lifelines through has made me feel much more in control of my future plans."

Assessing your aims

The following exercises are all about 'Assessment', the next step in the Balance Model. Your work-life balance is something that is always on

Your aims and lifeline(s)

	AIMS – WORK
1	
2	
3	

	AIMS – HOME
1	
2	
3	

	LIFELINE(S)

the move, there will be few times in your life when you can afford to sit back and tell yourself you have balanced living sorted out for the forseeable future. Something will come up, either at work or at home – it could be organizational change, it could be relationship issues, you may experience ill health for a time, eldercare demands that drop on you out of the blue, one or more of your children might have to change schools or your childcare arrangements might break down. At some points you can manage with small adjustments to your situation; at other times everything happens at once and you have to prioritize. You can't fix everything immediately – so this next exercise is a way of prioritizing your Aims.

Exercise

Take your six Aims and, on the checklist opposite, score them against the seven following criteria. If I achieve this Aim, will it:

• Make me happy?

• Improve my home life?

• Develop my work/career?

• Increase my finances?

• Enhance my health and well-being?

• Positively affect people at work and at home?

• Move me closer to my Lifeline Objectives?

For each statement that the Aim fulfils, score one point; score nothing if it won't achieve that goal. You might have to think quite carefully about this. For example, if you are going to work out at the gym twice a week it may not initially make you happy, but achieving your objective on a long-term basis should. If it takes time away from your family it might not improve your home life in the short term, but as you become more healthy and have more energy it should do so. Likewise, your additional health and well-being should contribute to your productivity and creativity at work, which in the long run should increase your finances, though the immediate cost of the gym membership may temporarily decrease them. The main objective is probably to enhance your health and well-being, which will ultimately positively affect those around you. Improving your health is unlikely to have a negative effect on any positive Lifeline Objective, but your choice of exercise and timing of work-out sessions could require some thought so as not to impinge on family time or work demands.

Note your Aims below, ticking the appropriate box and scoring 1 for every question you can answer 'Yes'.

Assess your aims

WILL MY WORK AIMS ...	Aim 1	Aim 2	Aim 3
Make me happy?			
Improve my home life?			
Develop my work/career?			
Increase my finances?			
Enhance my health?			
Positively affect people at work and home?			
Move me closer to my Lifeline Objective?			
TOTAL:			

WILL MY HOME AIMS ...	Aim 1	Aim 2	Aim 3
Make me happy?			
Improve my home life?			
Develop my work/career?			
Increase my finances?			
Enhance my health?			
Positively affect people at work and home?			
Move me closer to my Lifeline Objective?			
TOTAL:			

When you've scored them, pick your highest scoring Work Aim and Home Aim.

Whether you intuitively rated them in this order, the Aims with the highest scores are those which will make the most difference to the balance of your life and are therefore the ones you should start work on first.

Putting it all together

This is a good time to look at the opportunities currently available to you. Even small changes can open doors, both internal and external, and have far-reaching, knock-on effects. If you have now established a baseline for your material needs, identified the key needs and values of your emotional needs and looked at your tolerations and boundaries, you are now in a good position to look at those activities, experiences or aspirations in your work and home environments which excite, energize and empower you, which reflect your deepest beliefs and allow you to have your needs met. Equally, you can now see more clearly what aspects of work and home are having negative effects on your life.

Exercise

Fill in the following bumper checklist to see how you have summarized your life at a glance.

Where you are now and where you want to go

1	The differences between my current Balance Wheel and my ideal Balance Wheel showed me that:	....
2	My/our financial monthly baseline is:	....
3	The monthly/weekly time baseline I need for my personal commitments is:	....
4	I have committed to spending the following time (weekly/monthly) on my health and well-being:	....
5	I have resolved to do the following in the next (6/12 months) to promote my personal development:	....
6	My three key emotional needs that must be met on a long-term basis are:	1 .... 2 .... 3 ....

7	My three key values that I want to live by are:	1 .... 2 .... 3 ....
8	Three key tolerations I plan to deal with immediately are:	1 .... 2 .... 3 ....
9	My personal boundaries need to be moved in relation to the following:	1 .... 2 .... 3 ....
10	My three Work Aims, in order of importance, are:	1 .... 2 .... 3 ....
11	My three Home Aims, in order of importance, are:	1 .... 2 .... 3 ....
12	My Lifeline Objectives are:	1 .... 2 .... 3 ....

Extended exercise

When you put all the issues you have worked on in this chapter together, you may find that some of them need adjusting in relation to each other. Your Aims should fit in with getting your needs met and dealing with your tolerations. Your Lifelines should bear a strong relationship to the answer you gave to question 1 above, and to your key values.

The big decision

At this half-way point in the book, we hope you will have looked at: the influences on your perceptions of work and home; the way in which you use the two areas to build your personal identity; and the investments you have made in, and returns you are getting from, your current job. When you take these factors into account and re-read your 'Where you are now and where you want to go' checklist, you should be feeling ready to take what may be some major decisions in your life. These are now the questions you need to answer:

1   If you are currently working, is this the job/career that can (if it doesn't already) fulfil your material and emotional needs?

   (a) If the answer to that question is 'Yes, but …', what is it about your work that needs to change in order to provide you with a better balanced life? To help you find the answers and take action go to Chapter 4.

   (b) If the answer to question 1 is 'I'm still not sure', read Chapters 4 and 5 and see which options fit best with your needs.

   (c) If the answer is 'No', you may want to move directly to Chapter 5, which will give you a range of options from career changes to setting up your own business.

2   If you are not currently working, or you are in a job that you don't consider a long-term career, do you now have some ideas about what sort of work you would like to move into?

   (a) If the answer is 'Yes', Chapters 4 and 5 will provide you with some possible ways to approach a new career, from working flexibly for an employer to becoming self-employed.

   (b) If the answer is 'No', revisit the last three chapters with the more specific goal of identifying one or more areas which will fit comfortably or strike a chord with your needs and values. Then go to Chapter 5.

3 If the minor adjustments or major changes you anticipate making at work will still leave your home life lacking in balance, work through Chapters 4 and 5 and apply their ideas and principles to your home as well as work situation. Please also read Chapter 6, where we suggest a variety of resources you can draw on, from stress management techniques to advice on organizing your finances.

Marie

Marie was wondering whether she could stay working for the council, but as a self-employed person. "I can suddenly see a new way of life – or of work – opening up … But I've got to think it through before I start making suggestions. I'm very excited about the prospects, suddenly."

Anthony

Anthony decided that to give up on the bank would feel like failure, so he had to start turning it around and getting on top of the job. "I've got to get abreast of the new technology and start providing my customers with a better service. If I get made redundant then, well at least I've tried. Strangely enough, if I look at it like that, work starts to become a 'quest' again – one of my values."

Jonathan

Jonathan knew there was never a chance that he would give up nursing in the public sector, but faced the fact that he needed to make changes in his working arrangements and position with his colleagues.

Della

Della decided to do something that would allow her to develop her values and skills in home-making, creating good, comfortable environments for people to be in. "I'm still not sure whether this would be working for someone else, or my own business, which would be more exciting but also more frightening."

CHAPTER 4

Making work work for you

THIS CHAPTER COVERS:

- Your current job.

- You and your job – an important relationship: job description and roles.

- Workload and work organization – dealing with excessive workload, managing your time, getting organized.

- The Negatives – what's stopping you from making changes?

- Innovative work organization – innovative work options, picking the right option for you, making your case.

- Commitments, carrots and sticks.

If you're reading this chapter, you will have decided that either your current job or work situation is one you want to stick with, or that it's at least worth considering avoiding the major upheaval of a job or career change if you can just get a bit more balance between your work and home.

Exercise

Here's a quick checklist to remind you of how you feel about your job.
Again, tick the appropriate boxes.

Your current job

	GOOD	OK	POOR
The personal satisfaction I get from my job is:			
The amount of money I am paid is:			
The other financial benefits are:			
My relationships with my colleagues are:			
The way my work is managed is:			
My future career prospects are:			
My working conditions are:			
The hours I work are:			
The appreciation I get for my contribution is:			
The professional training I can access is:			
The personal development I can access is:			
My job security is:			
In comparison to others, my employer is:			
TOTALS:			

- If your highest total is the 'Good' column, there is a lot about your current employment that's worth hanging on to. We'll look at ways in which you can improve any areas which are 'OK' or downright 'Poor'.

- If your highest total is in the OK column, but you also had a few Goods, you still have plenty going for you in your present job. Keep reading to see whether you can't transform most of the OKs into Goods, and improve many of the Poors.

- If your highest total is in the Poor column, maybe you should think again about whether this is the job for you. Perhaps these are nearly balanced by the Goods, in which case it's worth working on the Poor and OK aspects to make this the right job for you right now.

You and your job – an important relationship

If, having done the checklist, you feel that on balance your current job has as many or more positive benefits than negative aspects, then it is certainly worth your while revisiting these. Remind yourself why you went into the job in the first place, what seemed exciting and stimulating about it and what you thought you could achieve. Were these expectations met? If so, are they still current and are there still goals that you want to achieve? If your original expectations were not met, consider why this might have been and whether it was to do with factors entirely beyond your control or whether, with a fresh awareness of your current Aims and over-arching Lifeline, you feel more empowered to make some changes which will help you achieve your original objectives. There are many ways in which you as an individual can act to make changes to your situation at work and we will look at those first. After that we'll turn our attention to ways in which you can work with your employer or manager to bring better balance to your life.

Anthony

> Anthony found that, despite how bad he felt about his work right now, thinking about why he went into the bank in the first place reminded him that there were a lot of good sides to working there. He also had to admit that the downturn in his job satisfaction was at least partly due to his failure to adjust to technical and workplace changes, which had the knock-on effects of worse relationships with his colleagues, less appreciation of his contribution and longer working hours. "I think they (senior management) could have communicated and handled the way our roles have had to change better; but perhaps it's fair to say that I haven't done my part either." He agreed that most of his colleagues, including those in his own age group, had learned the new technology and were managing their workloads and enjoying the new relationship with the customers. "I do still feel loyal to the bank and, although I didn't think my job would ever involve being so much of a salesman, I'd still rather be working there than anywhere else."

Your job description

When you applied for your current job, it was probably in response to a job description advertised either internally or externally. You must have felt that your interests, skills and experience were appropriate to this job description and so, presumably, did whoever took the decision to appoint you. In retrospect, though, was the original job description an accurate depiction of the role and tasks you were (or are now) expected to carry out? If it was not, or if your work has changed during the time you have been in the position, it could be useful to write yourself an up-to-date job description. When you have done this, check the differences between this and your official one; think about which you prefer. If there are substantial differences – and whether you are happy or unhappy with them – consider whether it would be useful to discuss them with your supervisor or line manager. Perhaps you are not getting enough recognition for the range of work you are doing, or perhaps you are doing tasks that you feel should not be part of your responsibilities. Either way, it may be time to update your official job description; this may make you feel more comfortable with your position within your team and/or the organization as a whole.

Marie

> Marie realized that her own job description hadn't been updated for a few years, and she found re-reading it quite an eye-opener. It didn't include all her current responsibilities and she felt she needed to think about how much of the role she wanted to continue with. "As director of human resources this has given me some pause for thought – I should be the one up-dating all staff job descriptions. This may be a task to be carried out organization-wide in the near future."

Your roles at work

Whether your organization is large or small, you will mainly be working with a specific group of colleagues; amongst whom you will be fulfilling two roles. Your most obvious role is that related to your job title and description – 'sales representative', 'production assistant', 'supervisor' or 'manager' etc. These job titles/descriptions are not only shorthand for describing your areas of responsibility but also your relationship with the rest of the team, including your place in the hierarchy and your level of experience and skills compared with the others.

When you are looking at your job description, take a moment to think about whether it reflects your relationship to your colleagues appropriately. Are you still labelled as a junior member of the team when in fact your length of service and the work you do has moved on since your role was originally defined? Or are you stuck in a narrow role and would like to increase the scope or change the area of your work? If this is the case, reflect on what you would ideally like your role to be and how you could achieve this.

But before approaching your line manager, think through how the team could operate around your changed role, what training you might require and how long you might take to get up to speed. It could also be helpful to talk to a trusted colleague about how they and others might feel about this change, and to consider how customers or clients would be affected. Not least, how would a change of role impact on your manager and even the organization as a whole? For example, your manager may have to spend more time supervising you in a new role, or it might be necessary to recruit someone else to fill your old position (whom you might need to train up). If you can demonstrate that you've calculated all these business and personal implications, you are more likely to be able to make a strong case for change and to answer any difficult questions about your proposal.

Apart from your 'work' role you will also be operating in a personal role among your immediate colleagues, and the way this role has developed may or may not be adding positively to how you feel about your job. For example, if your work role is one in which you support other team members, do they expect you to support them in personal ways as well? If you are responsible for the supervision of other colleagues, does this inhibit how you relate to them as people and make you feel isolated? Perhaps your age or personality has led others to regard you as the team carer, the coffee-maker, the problem-solver, the joker, the social organizer, or simply as 'difficult'. It's also possible that different members of your team, or people at different levels, see you in different roles and that you are constantly having to move between these expectations.

Take some time to reflect on how you seem to be perceived by others; consider how your role came about – perhaps it started when you were new in the job and wanted to make friends, or perhaps one colleague in particular has imposed this role on you. Decide whether you are happy to accept whatever your role may be among your team: there may be some very positive aspects to being seen as the social organizer of the group, or a problem-solver.

On the other hand, if you are sick of being expected to crack jokes or do the lunch run, it's time to make some changes. Next time colleagues ask you to make coffee, tell them you're in the middle of an important piece of work and suggest that the team has a roster for getting lunch. Go against expectations and make a thoughtful remark when a joke is what people clearly anticipate from you, or take a more measured approach the next time anyone expects you to react negatively to a new suggestion. Limit the time you spend listening to other people's problems if they're getting on top of you, and recommend other avenues they could pursue (eg calling the company's Employee Assistance Programme counselling line or seeing their doctor). If you can consciously maintain a different approach with colleagues over a few weeks they will quickly change their expectations of your behaviour and you can free yourself from performing a role which doesn't suit you.

Lisa

Lisa tried adopting a different approach, and found it worked. She was always asked to make the coffee, which she didn't mind when she wasn't busy and there was a meeting going on. "But the other day three of the others were sitting around chatting, and I was typing up a script with an urgent deadline. So when they said would I mind doing the coffees, I just kept typing, said I had to get the script finished and if someone was making it could I have a white coffee, no sugar. They looked a bit stunned, but I got my coffee – and then one of the girls got me a sandwich at lunchtime, which was good."

Workload and work organization

One of the commonest causes of work-life imbalance is excessive workload. Over the past decade or so most organizations have down-sized their workforce while trying to maintain the same or higher levels of productivity. Meeting or exceeding budget or productivity targets in one year often results in budget cuts and higher targets the following year. On top of this, more stringent measures around monitoring, evaluation and accountability have been introduced which usually demand more time. Constantly evolving communications technology has produced a number of negatives as well as positives, such as the huge numbers of e-mails people have to deal with, the expectation that workers are constantly available by phone, and the assumption that any of these communications can be dealt with instantly.

Dealing with excessive workload

If you are someone whose ability to balance their lives is compromised by a heavy and seemingly never-ending workload, you may have to discuss this with your manager; but there are some initial steps you can take on your own.

Exercise

A simple way of deciding whether the problem is one of too much work, or whether you are not working as effectively as you could, is to keep a time log for a couple of weeks. In your Balance Book, divide each day into 15-minute sections and, every hour, make a quick note of the activities you have covered and how much time you have spent on each. At the end of the day record your total hours worked and create a breakdown of activities. To speed up this process, you might want to work out a set of symbols or initials for the six or eight main activities you are involved in – but don't forget important ones such as thinking or organizing.

At the end of a week or so, when you add up the totals and summarize the activities under key headings, you will be able to identify what percentage of your time you spend on what. Identify whether and/or where you may be wasting time or working less productively by assessing whether there are things that take up significant or unnecessary amounts of your time without helping you achieve your goals. If, though, this exercise shows that you *are* working effectively most of the time, then the problem lies in the quantity of your workload, and that will have to be tackled through discussions with your manager or your whole team. At least, though, you will have some hard facts to present about your working time and outputs. Before you begin this discussion about your workload, however, take some time to consider whether you yourself may be the cause of the problem.

Are you actively taking on more work than you can realistically cope with? You might be doing this because:

• of a genuine interest in and commitment to your job;

- you feel that working long hours is the only way to demonstrate commitment or gain experience that will take you up the career ladder;

- you feel you are not performing well and have to work the extra hours to compete with colleagues;

- client/customer demand is high and neither you nor your manager has confronted this issue;

- you have taken on a 'martyr' role among your colleagues, and choose to be seen as the over-worked team member.

Then again, you may be passively accepting work that is given to you because you feel unable to say No through fear or guilt. If this is you, have another look at the section on tolerations and boundaries in Chapter 3, and consider including in your Work Aims being more assertive about not taking on excess workload.

Naomi

Naomi thought of herself as an efficient worker, but realized she hadn't been organizing things as well as she thought. She spent long periods in the lab, but then also had to write up reports and supervise other members of her team, and carry out general administration.

She had been in the habit of taking regular tea breaks, but using the time to check e-mails and voice mail and reply to the most urgent. Then she would go back to what she had been doing with a broken chain of thought, only half the e-mails and messages dealt with and feeling oppressed by the rest. She started taking proper breaks, making specific times for dealing with e-mails and messages, and working a day a week at home to write up reports in peace, instead of the constant interruptions of the office. "Of course I'm available by phone or e-mail if people need me urgently, but they seem to respect my time working at home more than if I'm there in person. I'm getting through work more quickly and I feel less hassled."

If you are responsible for work distribution, take a look at your delegation skills. Are you spending an unnecessary amount of time on work that could more effectively be done by someone else? If you feel this could be you, think about why you are acting like this. It could be because you don't trust your colleagues, in which case you are both undermining their confidence and depriving them of the opportunity to develop. Although it may initially take time to train another person to do new tasks, in the long term you will gain time.

It may be that you are trying to impress your own line manager with the amount of work you take on. Hopefully, they would be more impressed by your effective workload management and ability to delegate to your team. Perhaps you yourself fear that your team will react badly to being given more work. Teams who are able to organize work distribution among themselves, and are trusted to carry out that work on their own terms, have been shown to perform more productively, co-operatively and in a trustworthy manner. Two key rules of delegation are: to communicate clearly and specifically *what*, *how* and in what *timeframe* the task is to be done; and having delegated the job, to let the person get on with it without frequent checks from you, although they should know they can come back to you for help or information at any time. People learn best from their own mistakes and some positive guidance at the end of the task will be far more effective than constant interference.

Marie

> Marie didn't think she was a control freak, but did sometimes slip into thinking she was indispensable and could do everything best. "It was only when I thought up my game plan, and started consciously to groom my deputy director as my successor, that I realized how very good she was, and that sometimes she excelled in areas where I was not so good." Marie then saw that this attitude could cascade down the department, and that everyone benefited – taking on more responsible work so getting better job satisfaction, learning new skills and freeing up the people above them from tasks they didn't need to be doing.

Managing your time

As we know all too well, there are only 24 hours in a day and not one of us can stretch a week beyond seven days, no matter how much the demands on our time would seem to require it. While many of us are racing around frantically, constantly worrying how we are going to get everything done and feeling harassed at the end of the day because we didn't, there are some people who manage to fit more in and seem less stressed about life. If you are one of the first group and would rather be one of the second, here are some tips on how to join the serenely productive.

Getting organized

One of the secrets of productive people is preparation. They plan in advance, prioritize tasks and have effective systems in place both at work and home. You may not be someone who can maintain complex filing and other systems, but there are some very simple and effective ways of organizing your time, dealing with paperwork and staying on top of administration.

Your balance diary – for work, home or both

Buy an A4, page-a-day office diary (do this, even if it's the last quarter of the year) and keep it on your desk or where you work. As you come to them, fold each page in half lengthwise, and write work commitments and plans in the resulting left-hand column and home tasks in the right-hand column. This is your 'Balance Diary'. First, go through any other diaries or birthday books you have and transfer all work and home events, birthdays, anniversaries etc into your Balance Diary. You might want to consider including reminders to yourself on earlier dates, such as 'Buy and post card for dad's birthday'; 'Get suit cleaned for presentation on Friday'.

At the end of each day, list all your tasks for the next day in the appropriate columns. Check daily your other personal or work diaries for any appointments or reminders and write them into your Balance Diary. When you start work the next day, rank your tasks in order of importance – you might want to invest in a set of coloured pens or find other ways of coding the priority of each task. Set aside a specific time early in the day to carry out these tasks (perhaps after dealing with the most immediate phone messages, e-mails or post, or other routine meetings you may have to attend first thing). As you complete each task, tick it off in your Balance Diary. Starting the day with a sense of achievement produces a more positive frame of mind than working all day with tasks you haven't done hanging over you. Transfer any tasks you haven't achieved that day to the following day's list. If one or more tasks are constantly transferred to the next day, either it is not that important, so write it in a week or month ahead when it will have become important, delete it entirely or give it top priority the next day and make sure you do it.

When you enter an appointment in your Balance Diary, give it a finish time as well as a start time and stick to it. Allocate weekly time for administrative or organizational tasks that you usually avoid, and try to ensure uninterrupted time for thinking, writing and planning. Before you make one of your listed phone calls, or have a meeting, make sure that you have all the information to hand that you or the other person will need and, where possible, let others know what you will need from them. If you have memos, reports or other documents that you will need for a meeting or phone call, file them in the correct date page of your Balance Diary so they are to hand at the right time.

Make notes of all your phone conversations, phone numbers, reference numbers and other things you need to remember. Use the Balance Diary as your brain dump – everything you need to find later should be in there somewhere, even if you transfer the information to other places as well. When bills, memos, invitations, reminders, letters to be answered come in, file them in your Balance Diary in the date page on which you have to deal with them. Pay, answer or respond to them at the same time as you carry out your other listed tasks for the day, if you can do this at work. Or put them aside to deal with in a break or keep a special folder inside your bag or briefcase to take items which have to be dealt with that evening home with you. Use the same folder, or another one, to bring things from home to be filed in your Balance Diary at work and make sure the first thing you do on arrival at each place is unload and file or deal with the items. Alternatively, if you want to keep work and home entirely separate, keep a Balance Diary in each place.

Della

Della had been running a diary like this at home for years, and claimed it was only because of this that people thought she was efficient and well-organized. "I started one at the real estate agency when I first went there and, because I'm only part-time, it meant that whoever was on reception when I wasn't knew exactly what needed doing and had the right documents on the right day. I also used it to tell the other receptionists what I'd done during my shifts, and they started doing the same." She was well known in her family for never forgetting birthdays, but said it was not because she had a good memory, just a good system.

Your paper-free desk

Buy or requisition a stacker for your desk with at least four compartments. This is the end of untidy piles of paper, lost memos and that feeling of being surrounded by chaos. Mark the top tray of your stacker 'Today'. In it, put all the papers, letters, memos, reports etc that you have to deal with urgently. As you leave your desk for the day, put all the papers which have to be dealt with tomorrow (including those you have filed in advance in your Balance Diary) in this top tray; list them, along with tomorrow's other tasks, in your Balance Diary. Your 'Today' tray should be empty by the end of each day; if an item keeps going back into it move it into your second tray down, which is your 'Monday' tray. In this compartment, file all papers which can wait for a week before being dealt with. Every Monday (or whichever day of the week you choose) make your first task (listed in your Balance Diary) to go through this tray and re-file those tasks which need to be dealt with that day or within the week, those which can wait another week and those which can be held over indefinitely or until they are activated by someone or something else. These latter can be filed in your third tray, which you can label 'Pending'. Your work may require you to add some more trays to your stacker for particular types of paperwork, but your bottom tray, labelled 'Miscellaneous' or 'Various', is your catch-all for everything else that clutters up your desk and gets in the way of concentrating on the task in hand. If all else fails, you should be able to find that lost memo or report someone asked you to read in your bottom compartment.

Your home (or work) filing system

What do you do with all those old bills you've paid, receipts you feel you ought to keep, insurance policies, guarantees and service agreements for household appliances, advertising flyers for services that you might want one day, credit card bills and tickets that might be useful for your tax returns? If, like many people, they go into various files, boxes or drawers, or you end up throwing them out when the pile becomes too high, here's a simple way to keep organized.

Buy an expanding or accordion file with alphabetically marked pockets. File all your paid bills, receipts etc in this, under basic headings you know you'll remember. For instance, your Visa bills might live on their own in the 'V' section, but 'W' might contain your water rates, the receipt, guarantee and service plan for your washing machine and directions to your friend Wendy's new house. When you can't remember the name of the plumbing company whose flyer claimed they were reasonable and efficient, you'll only have to sift through your postal receipts, parking fines and payroll slips to find them instead of a whole load of different places you might have stored it. You can keep one of these going for years, or you can time limit them and start a new one for each calendar or tax year. This idea could be useful at work if you have to manage a lot of hard-to-file paperwork.

Ed

Ed used a similar, but smaller, filing system with days of the week instead of alphabetical compartments. "Because I'm always on the move between clients, and I don't always get back into the office every day, I have to have the right hard copy documentation with me for the week. I just take everything I'll need for the next week and shove it into 'Monday', 'Tuesday', 'Wednesday' … then I know I'm covered." Although he could always be faxed or e-mailed wherever he was, Ed said there were always some bits of paper he needed that weren't in the database and he wasted less of other people's time by being organized.

These three suggestions are all very simple ways of organizing aspects of your life – you can probably think up others that will complement or add to them, or that may suit your work and home life better. What they demonstrate, though, is that some basic organizational strategies will make a considerable difference to your time management and stress levels – which always rise when you feel out of control. Without resorting to complex systems or spending valuable time on advance planning, you can train yourself to form good working habits which allow you to be more in control of your time and paperwork.

Judith, returning to work at 45

"Four years ago I reassessed my work-life balance, pruning tasks where necessary and changing how I spent the larger part of each week. Yes, I cut back on the time spent with a husband, three children, an aged, live-in mother-in-law, two cats, two guinea pigs, a hamster, the youth club with its associated committees, and a group of refugee women to whom I was teaching English. The liberated time gave me a tremendous sense of freedom and, most importantly, the opportunity to do something for me – I returned to work after a 15-year career break.

"It was with some trepidation that I re-entered the role of employee. I need not have worried. I recaptured the professional part of me that had remained dormant, hidden and unused behind the all-pervasive 'mummy/wife/carer' role. The one thing I felt equipped to do was juggle, and indeed this was one of my most precious transferable skills. Within a couple of weeks of being accepted as a visiting university lecturer I also began work for a charity. Two part-time jobs that more than filled my desire to 'do something for myself'.

"My initial happiness, however, was mirrored by my children's distress; no longer was I always on hand to do essential and non-essential chores, to provide unlimited amounts of emotional support and to be there 'just in case'. We coped. The longer I have been working the easier it has become. My employers – and my husband – are understanding and flexible should the children fall ill etc. Routines have evolved; these centre around daily lists that tell the children where I am, what I'm doing, when I will be home and what I expect them to have done by the time I come home. This latter usually involves the elder two feeding themselves and the pets while keeping an eye on the youngest when he returns from the childminder. I would not now return to my pre-work existence. We eat as nutritionally but not everything is home prepared. Sometimes I am tired, but probably less irritable, and the house is as it always was – clean but messy. On those occasions when I feel beset with tasks (usually marking exam scripts) I know the pressure is transient and the benefits of having some 'me time' outweigh any temporary stress."

The negatives – what's stopping you from making changes?

We've just looked at some changes you can make to how you organize your home and work life. They are pretty easy to do and the question to ask yourself is why have you not done them, or something like them, before now. This is the subject of the next exercise in the Balance Model which explores the 'Negatives' – the barriers each of us have to overcome in bringing balance to our lives.

Exercise

Take another look at the top three Work and Home Aims you identified in Chapter 3 (you might want to revise or add some Aims around the tips for better work and time management outlined above; if so, don't forget to run them through the 'Assess your aims' checklist and rank them against your existing ones). If you believe your Aims will make a significant difference to your life, why have you not started working towards them, let alone achieved them, already? The answer is because there's always a set of Negatives which make it seem too hard. Some of these Negatives will be in the outside world – in the workplace, at home; others will be inside your head. Attitudes such as 'I'm no good at …'; 'Nothing I do makes any difference …'; or 'They'd never agree to …'

Take your top Work and Home Aims (or work through more) and list the Negatives (generated from your workplace, your home and yourself) that are stopping you moving forward. When you have done this, your task is to come up with practical ways in which you can start overcoming each Negative.

Negatives

Work Aim 1:	
NEGATIVES	**WAYS TO OVERCOME**
At work	
•	•
•	•
•	•

At home	
• • •	• • •
Own attitudes • • •	• • •

Home Aim 1: _____

_____

NEGATIVES	WAYS TO OVERCOME
At work • • •	• • •
At home • • •	• • •
Own attitudes • • •	• • •

Extended exercise

In your Balance Book write some more about each of the Negatives you have identified. For each one, write something about:

- When did this Negative start?

- Who was involved in affirming this Negative?

- What has been your own role in affirming this Negative?

- Are there aspects of this Negative that are outside your control – really?

When you have spent some time answering these questions, look at the ways to overcome the Negatives you have suggested on the check-list. Now write some more about these suggestions (prompted by the questions below) in your Balance Book:

- Why is this a good first step to overcoming the Negative?

- If this one works, what will I do next?

- How will I feel when I have taken these steps?

- Do I really believe I can achieve them?

Jonathan

> Jonathan's first work aim was to talk to his team about his needs for balancing work and home. He hadn't done so before because he was afraid they'd see his kind of lifestyle as less important than theirs, his dog as less valuable than their children, his training needs as selfish and ambitious. He felt that he was to blame for making these assumptions, and that because he had always offered to cover for colleagues with childcare

problems they thought it was OK with him to go on doing this. In fact, he interpreted his colleagues asking for cover as them not valuing him as a whole person. "My first step to overcoming this had to be talking openly about my needs, just as they did about theirs. If that was accepted, I'd be able to say more about work organization. I thought I would feel better when I'd taken these steps, but not as good as I actually did feel."

Jonathan spoke to his closest colleague, Annie, first. She was amazed that he hadn't said anything before and offered to back him up in a team meeting if he needed it. As it turned out, everyone was equally supportive and they ended up arranging a new roster system so that everyone put in their preferred working hours at the beginning of each month and everyone compromised around each other's needs. It turned out that a rostering software package was on order for the whole hospital, which would make the process even simpler. "There was a public holiday last week that no one wanted to work, so we agreed that we would each come in for a couple of hours, then no one would lose a whole day and no one would feel hard done by. We told the patients what was happening and it turned out to be a really happy day for all of us."

Jonathan now had his training course back on track, he was able to walk Max enough for his neighbour to do the rest and he felt a great sense of achievement in having taken some control over the balance of his life. It hadn't meant huge changes, but the effects had been considerable.

Christopher, finding balance while not working

"I loved my job, even though it sometimes meant long hours and a fair bit of stress. I'd just got to a position where I thought my experience was paying off, and as a specialist in the IT industry I was secure and in a position to keep moving onwards and upwards. And then I was made redundant. The whole industry slowed down and my company no longer needed people like me who specialized in investment-heavy, big, international projects. It was a real shock and hard to come to terms with – especially as the job had a big social component; suddenly all that was gone as well. I went on meeting up with ex-colleagues for a time, but it got a bit depressing.

"From having difficulty finding enough time for home and family I suddenly found myself in the opposite position, and not sure what to do with myself at home all day. For the first couple of months I worked on the garden, pretty sure that I'd be employed again soon. But nothing was coming up, so I had to rethink for the longer term. My wife took on more work to keep us afloat, so I did more with the house and children – but I needed more than that. I decided to get into a personal fitness routine and now head off to the gym first thing everyday, which helps me to get going in the morning. And I am a lot fitter than I was before. I'm now also doing some unpaid work for voluntary organizations and friends, who need but cannot afford to pay for IT skills. That keeps my skills honed and I can put them on my CV instead of having a gap of several months. And I'm doing research and retraining in a couple of new areas which I will pursue if I don't secure any employment in the next couple of months. But I'm still hoping that, with persistence, I will get a job in the area that I know best "

Innovative work organization

The first half of this chapter has looked at ways in which you as an individual can influence different aspects of your current job to bring better balance to your work and home life. However small these adjustments may be, they can produce a ripple effect in your personal ability to organize your time, tasks and commitments, with far-reaching and positive outcomes. However, there are other aspects of your work which you cannot tackle without enlisting the help of your employer, your manager and/or colleagues. These revolve around the pattern and hours of your work, and where you do it.

Some of the most helpful ways in which organizations can help their employees to balance their lives is to offer them flexible working arrangements or leave options. These work best where the employer understands that allowing people to work flexibly is not an accommodation they have to make for someone with problems at home, but a policy which helps them to achieve their business objectives. Many businesses who do appreciate this will have a range of good policies in place, which they may call 'work-life balance', 'family friendly' or 'flexible working' policies. If your employer is one of these, your first step will be to get hold of a copy of the appropriate policy handbook from the department which deals with staff contracts etc (Human Resources, Corporate Affairs) or access it on the company intranet. If you are lucky enough to be employed by one of the leading best practice organizations, they will have an extensive range of options for you to choose from. Others will be less liberal, but sometimes for perfectly valid operational reasons. Here, though, is a summary of the most commonly offered innovative working options, with some of the positive results they can have for both you and your employer.

Innovative work options

Flexitime

Flexible working hours or flexitime schemes allow you to choose (sometimes within limits of 'core times') the times you start and finish work. They also allow you to carry over excess or deficit hours beyond an accounting period (usually monthly), with the option of taking 'flexileave'.

Benefits to your employer
Benefits to your employer include recruiting and retaining staff; reducing payment on overtime hours and minimizing absenteeism. They will also benefit from creating a greater sense of responsibility and commitment from you and other employees, and from improvements in time management and efficiency. Flexitime can enable businesses to match working hours with peaks and troughs of output and with extended opening hours.

Benefits to you
Benefits to you include fitting working hours around home responsibilities, particularly if you're working long hours or have caring responsibilities. It also allows you to deal with personal matters, such as dentist or doctor visits, out of work hours.

Compressed working week
Squeezing a full-time job into a shorter working week is growing in popularity. Examples include working four long days instead of five, doing a nine-day fortnight, or shortening breaks during the day and leaving earlier.

Benefits to your employer
Benefits to your employer may include more flexible hours to meet customer expectations; more flexible office space; better staff recruitment and retention, and other benefits similar to those of flexitime.

Benefits to you

Benefits to you are also similar to those for flexitime, but could include giving you a regular day off per week or fortnight.

Part-time work

A part-time worker is defined in UK government statistics as someone who works for less than 30 hours a week. However, the UK's Trade Union Congress found that 14% of part-time workers described themselves as 'part-time' while working more than 30 hours. Two thirds of part-time workers work less than 21 hours a week and the average number of hours worked is 18 for women and 16 for men.

The most common reason for employing part-time workers is to achieve flexibility of cover. The next most important factors are the need for work to be done only at particular times and the need to provide cover at peak times.

Part-time work can offer you the opportunity to work reduced hours around caring responsibilities, and can help you pursue education, leisure and other activities. If you are thinking of reducing your hours from full-time to part-time, remember to check the impact of this on your pension, and how your employer will view your future career path.

Voluntary reduced work time or V-time

'V-time' schemes allow you voluntarily to trade income for time off. You are given the option of reducing full-time working hours (usually by between 5%–50%) for a specified period, say a year, with the right to return full-time at the end of that period.

A reduction in hours can provide organizations with the flexibility to redirect personnel savings to critical project needs, including hiring short-term employees.

V-time programmes might be a good option for you if you are having to deal with a temporary problem, doing a course or have some other time-limited interest or commitment.

Marie

It took Marie about six months to put everything in place before she submitted her proposal to senior management. She wanted to reduce her work at the council to half time, and for that time to be organized flexibly. Also, she asked them to second her for an extra day a week to a local voluntary organization which supported young people with disabilities and was badly in need of some support in managing its paid and volunteer personnel. Marie outlined to senior management the benefits of this arrangement, and explained that if they did not agree to the proposal they ran the risk of losing her services and experience altogether. (She had to be very sure she could go through with this if they turned her down; she checked that her savings would support her for six months while she found another job.) Marie told the managers that her deputy director was in a position to take over most of her role (with Marie as an advisor) and that this would enhance her value to the council. Marie also told the managers that her experience would grow on secondment, and that they could receive positive publicity from this arrangement as they could exploit her involvement in the golf competitions she intended to spend the rest of her time on.

"I think that it was because my proposal was so well researched, backed up and written in such detail that the senior management couldn't say No (see p. 139). I even had a random sample of 'internal clients' – staff from other departments who use our department as a resource – who said they would be happy with the new working arrangement I proposed. Anyway, we're three months into it now, and I'm a changed person. I'm enjoying every part of my life now, and I have so much more enthusiasm and energy for the old job, as well as the new one. What's more, the department is running at least as smoothly as when I was there full time!"

Job sharing

Job sharing is a way of working where two people voluntarily share the responsibilities, the pay, holidays and other benefits of one full-time job. There are now a wide range of jobs shared at all levels, including doctors, chief executives, probation officers, social workers, police officers, architects and planners.

Your employer could gain by doubling the input of skills and experience to one position, and knowing there is always cover for sickness and holidays. Job-sharers are often more productive than a single person, and can come up with creative solutions to a range of issues.

Job sharing can make it easier for women to return after maternity leave and can improve work opportunities for men and women carers of adults and children. To make a job share work well, though, you must be organized, communicate well with each other and establish excellent 'hand over' practices.

Annualized hours

Annualized hours is a system whereby the period of time within which you do your work is defined over a whole year. The actual dates and times that you work within that period should be organized to suit both your employer's – and your own – needs.

Your employer will gain flexibility through you working annualized hours, and it is often brought in as part of an overall restructuring. If your job has busy and less busy periods during the year, annualized hours can help match working time to need, reduce or abolish over-time and maximize productivity and efficiency.

You could use this scheme to work around home commitments such as school holidays, if this fits in with business peaks and troughs.

Home-/tele-working

Tele-working (or home-working) is defined as work that you do at home for your employer, or to sell to another person, and includes 'out-working' and people working partly from home.

There are direct cost advantages for your employer in savings on office space and several studies have indicated that people who work at home are up to 30% more efficient than office-based employees. This may be a result of the planning and management possible with home-based work, the lack of interruptions and the time gained from not travelling to and from work.

For some people, working at home full-time is a perfect arrangement, particularly if you have a long journey into work, move further away from your office or have a disability. For others, home-working on a part-time (eg a day a week) or occasional (eg to produce reports or other work that benefits from no interruptions, or to work while waiting for a service engineer to make a home visit) basis is prefer-able. Don't forget to consider the needs of others in your household who may have their own schedules while you are normally at work, and bear in mind that you may miss the social interaction with colleagues.

Hannah, part-time working single mother

"I was working 20 hours a week at my present job. I started at 9.30am and finished at 1.30pm every day. This seemed ideal until I realized that my work was piling up and I started to work longer hours and accrue lieu time.

"My boss (the only other person in the admin office) was going through a difficult stage and kept taking time off, which in turn meant I was working longer hours to cover in the office and wasn't having the chance to take the time owed to me. My children were neglected, they were not eating properly. They were snacking and then not hungry when I returned home to prepare a meal for them. We could not organize proper meals together and my housework was out of control. It was chaotic in the house and I was constantly 'chasing my tail' and getting stressed out. Everybody seemed unhappy. I found I was not relaxing at all or sitting down until 10.30 at night; usually I just collapsed into bed – exhausted!

"Through this experience, however, we identified that I was achieving so much more by working a chunk of longer hours instead of spreading my time out. When things returned to normal, and I was allowed to take my lieu time on Fridays, it was decided that I would work five hours for four days a week so that I could take Fridays off to get things done at home.

"Over time, and with better management (the previous boss left!) and office cover, I am now down to three full days a week – still working 20 hours. This means that one day I only take a half-hour lunch break. I work 9.30am–5.00pm Monday to Wednesday and have Thursday and Friday free to do my housework, shopping/washing etc; and I have the weekends off. I find that I achieve so much more at work doing full days and I am able to keep up to date with my typing; I am much less stressed. I am able to socialize with the staff, attend meetings and keep communication up (this is important when working part time as you can start to feel on the periphery, not part of the team). Team meetings have been re-scheduled to 9.30 on Monday mornings so I can attend.

"My home work is to a certain degree dictated by the weather. If it is fine, then I go out in the garden and get the washing done. If it's raining, I clean and tidy the house, answer e-mails, cook, iron and do paperwork/file etc. At the weekends I try to take the children out for a meal (if they're available), answer correspondence, and most importantly, relax.

"The one thing I haven't been able to achieve so far is having the time for a hobby. I did attend college for two years doing an 'A' Level in English, which I passed. This was extremely hard work and entailed long hours of homework and studying. It was worth the effort, but I gave myself additional pressure when circumstances changed at work and I was working extra hours. I am now attending night school on Mondays (6.00–8.30pm) learning woodwork (no homework). This will teach me how to make things for the garden, a useful hobby! I need to give myself permission to leave the housework and go to the gym or swimming pool. I plan to use the evenings more and not just collapse after clearing away the dishes. I would like to attend a cookery class but will only take on one course at a time, so I'm not over-committed.

"My children may be teenagers (and don't really take much notice of me), but they love it when I am at home on a Thursday and Friday evening. On Mondays I ask them to cook a microwave dinner or eat up plated leftovers from the previous Sunday. But on Tuesdays I tell them to wait for me and I cook for us all for 6.00pm. It is important to eat together as a family and establish a kind of routine. I am trying to keep this routine going, but everyone must remain flexible as circumstances are changing all the time."

Term-time working
Term-time working allows you to remain on a permanent contract as either a full- or part-time employee, but gives you the right to (unpaid) leave of absence during the school holidays.

Your employer could retain valuable experience within the business by enabling women returners and other parents to continue working, often full-time during school terms, and part-time working can be an asset to seasonally-based production.

If you are a working parent and have difficulty arranging care for some of the school holidays, this will enable you to balance work and home responsibilities without too much stress, and in some cases allow you to work where you otherwise might not have been able to at all.

Employment/career breaks
An employment or career break is an extended period of unpaid leave from your work. The intention is that you will return to work with your employer at an agreed date at the level or job you held previously, retaining all or most of the service-related benefits. This is sometimes called a 'retainer' or 're-entry' scheme, and it works best when you and you employer keep in touch during the break to ease re-entry.

This arrangement could benefit your employer because you are likely to return to work with the new experience and skills you have gained through higher education, training or other learning opportunities, without having to be paid while you achieve them.

A career break could allow you the security of knowing that you can return to a job after taking a specific break to do something significant for yourself, such as travel, education, volunteer work, looking after children beyond maternity or paternity leave, or caring for an elderly or sick relative.

Sabbaticals

Sabbatical leave is a period of time off in addition to annual leave, on full pay, awarded on the basis of length of service. It is usually a 'reward' for long service, which would enable you to take time out to recharge your batteries or study for a qualification.

Again, this helps your employer to retain your skills and experience and to recruit new staff. In the US and Australia, sabbaticals have been seen as part of personal growth and career development, and therefore a part of organizational learning. Recently, more businesses have been developing sabbaticals as a morale booster to deal with the costly problems of employee stress or burn-out.

Other leave options (which vary between companies, and indeed countries) include Maternity, Paternity and Adoption Leave, and Pay and Parental Leave. Also, Emergency Leave, Domestic Leave and Carer Leave. All tend to be short periods of either paid or unpaid leave that some organizations allow employees to take when personal emergencies occur. Countries in the European Union have legislated to make Parental Leave and Emergency Leave a statutory right.

Picking the right option for you

If you are going to make a successful application to your employer to change your working pattern, hours or place of work (and especially if the organization doesn't actively promote such options), you will have to produce a well-thought out and meticulously researched proposal. Your first step is to work out which of the above options, or which of the options offered by your employer, will achieve not only your needs but also the needs of the business. For example, if your job includes responsibility for answering phones or seeing customers between specified hours, requesting part-time hours or term-time working which don't cover these requirements will not get a favourable response. However, a job-share arrangement might not only help you to balance your commitments but might also give your employer more coverage and flexibility.

It may be that you will have to challenge a widely-held perception or aspect of workplace culture. Many service organizations are fearful of losing clients or customers if staff are not constantly available to take calls, attend meetings or deal with requests. This can often be a misplaced worry, especially as more client/customer organizations have their own work-life balance policies and appreciate them in other companies they deal with. If you work in such an environment and would like, for example, to work from home one day a week, you are much more likely to get a positive response if you have already worked out how you could be contacted by clients on that day (mobile phone, e-mail), and checked out with clients themselves whether they would find such an arrangement acceptable.

It may be that what you need to achieve better balance between yourself and your organization is not to do with changing your work arrangements, but is to do with developing your career by accessing training, applying for promotion or a different job. Applying for any of these options will require the same approach: thinking through a strong business case for your employer or manager, researching the attitudes of those it will affect, and being ready to answer challenging questions and compromise around the needs of others.

Making your case

The more time and effort you invest in preparing your proposal or application, the better your chance of getting a positive response. Here are some suggestions as to how to structure, and what to include in, your proposal.

1 Your current situation

Set out your name, job title and description, your current working hours/pattern/place.

2 Your proposed work option

State your proposed working arrangement (eg part-time working, annualized hours) and detail the hours/pattern/place of the new arrangement.

You might want to set out the above two answers in a table like the one below.

DAYS	Hours (current)	Hours (requested)	On-site (where)	Off-site (where)
Sunday				
Monday				
Tuesday				
Wednesday				
Thursday				
Friday				
Saturday				
Total weekly hours:				

3 Timing of the proposed arrangement

State when you would like the new arrangement to begin and, if it has a time limit, when it will finish.

4 Presenting the business case

(a) How will the proposed arrangement enhance – or at least sustain – your ability to get your job done?

- Explain how your proposed arrangement adds value to the business.

- Provide evidence of how you will contribute as much, if not more, with your new arrangement. Be specific.

- Consider broad gains such as reduced stress, decreased absenteeism and improved punctuality.

- At a minimum, show why the arrangement will not harm the business. A sample response for this question might be: "My annualized hours will allow me to work more hours during busy periods and not waste time in the office at less busy times".

(b) Describe any additional benefits to your organization that might result from this flexible working arrangement/break from work.

- Provide examples of how the arrangement will improve your ability to support the organization.

- Give specific examples, such as increased revenue, lowered payroll costs, decreased premises costs etc. A sample response for this question might be: "My five day, 9am–3pm, part-time week will allow me to maintain daily contact with my clients, plus it will be a developmental opportunity for a more junior person".

5 Confronting the issues
What problems could the new arrangement raise with:

(a) External customers/clients?
(b) Internal customers/clients?
(c) Your team/colleagues?
(d) Your manager?

- For each category think how your new arrangement will change your working relationship.

- Identify or suggest any possible problems, including obvious ones (eg not being in on Mondays) as well as more subtle ones (eg the ability of your manager to assess your performance when you are working at home). An example might be: "I won't be in the office to cover emergencies for my key project".

How to overcome any problems with each of these groups:

- For each of the groups listed, provide concrete solutions for any problems listed.

- Ideally, provide several possible solutions for each problem.

- Suggest alternatives that will meet the needs of the organization as well as all the individuals involved. A sample response for this question might be: "On Mondays I'll ring in to collect my voice mail and return any urgent calls from home".

6 Assessing and reviewing your performance
(a) Describe how you and your manager will assess whether your performance in your new working arrangement is meeting, or exceeding, targets.

- Develop or adapt clear and definite goals for effectively performing your job.

- Suggest timescales for delivering key pieces of work.

- Agree with your manager what qualities and behaviours constitute performing well in your job. A sample response might be: "I will continue to meet all expectations for my performance plan. I will also use the better focus of my home-working days to write up reports 5% more quickly".

(b) Specify a review process that you and your manager could constructively use to monitor and improve your flexible working arrangement.

- If there is a standard performance-tracking process in your organization, use that as a starting point.

- Develop a measurement plan that includes timescales and specific performance standards for yourself.

- Think about developing a performance measure which works for all key stakeholders – external customers/clients, internal customers/clients, your team/colleagues and your manager. Try to find a way to answer the question: "What would my manager consider to be a successful performance arrangement?"

- Involve the above stakeholders in developing your performance measures – ask trusted colleagues and even clients/customers to help you with this. A sample response for this question might be: "To begin with I will rely on our performance evaluation process to develop measurements for my new working arrangements. I would like to meet with my manager to assess my performance six weeks, and then three months, after I have started working in a job share".

7 Keeping tabs on the new working arrangement

• What would be an early warning sign that the arrangement wasn't working out?

• Think about and respond to worst case scenarios.

• Consider the possible negative effects of the arrangement on your team members, external and internal clients/customers and your manager. At what point would these negative effects make the arrangement unworkable?

• What would be the signs that the arrangement wasn't working? A sample response for this question might be: "I will know that my arrangement is unsuccessful if customer complaints increase because I am inaccessible".

If you can write a proposal for a new working arrangement that looks at all of these issues, and how you would deal with them, you will have answered in advance most of the negative questions that will be put to you. You will also have proven that you have the interests of your employer at heart, and have thought seriously about what these changes could mean to all parts of the organization. If you think such a proposal would be unnecessarily detailed to achieve the results you want, only use the suggestions you think are relevant to your situation. Still, you could usefully think through the answers to the other questions in case you are asked to respond to them verbally.

If you can successfully modify your own organizational and time management and/or adjust your working patterns around your home commitments and interests, you should be able to achieve a far greater degree of balance in your work and home life within your present job.

Anthony

Anthony didn't write out a full proposal, but then he wasn't actually asking for a dramatic change. He thought through all the issues around working with clients and colleagues (and his own manager) before making an appointment to see his boss. Anthony decided that he had nothing to lose by being honest, so he explained that he was having trouble with the new IT, was getting behind and, because he was still very committed to the bank, wanted to go on a couple of the training courses again to sort things out. It turned out that Anthony's manager had planned to talk to him about this in his next appraisal anyway, but this would have been a negative discussion with Anthony on the defensive.

Anthony went on a couple of intensive training courses and took some leave to get himself together before going back in to deal with clients. "My son Rob has been really helpful with the computer work; he's gone through things I didn't quite understand in class, and it's changed our relationship for the better. Della, my wife, has offered to help me organize my work schedule and I've gone on to medication for high blood pressure, which means I feel better physically now. Della and I have also joined the local gym and we're going on a weekend to a health farm next month." Anthony knows there is still a chance he'll be made redundant by the bank; "But at least I'll have done my best and gained some new skills in the process."

Exercise

Commitments – using carrots and sticks to stay committed to your aims

The next step in the Balance Model is looking at ways of staying committed to the Aims and Lifeline Objectives you have identified. For this exercise you will need to focus deeply on your own life and feelings in order to connect with the things that will really make you commit to achieving your Aims. This exercise requires some sustained time on your own.

Find a quiet place to sit, where you won't be disturbed for half an hour or so. Pick either your principal Work or Home Aim to start on, and ask yourself: "How will my life be more balanced if I achieve this Aim?" Close your eyes and visualize yourself one, two or perhaps five or more years from now. Project yourself forward to the time you have selected and imagine (in detail) how your life could be if you have achieved this Aim. Look at the effects on your work life, your home life, yourself and your relationships. See how far reaching these could be; something quite small could have a really big ripple effect. For example, perhaps your main Home Aim was to ask your partner and children for more help with domestic chores. In two years time this small step could have developed into a position where your children are more confident, self-sufficient and caring people than you might have expected. Your partner might have developed a greater respect for the work you do in the home, and it could have resulted in both of you re-negotiating your working hours on a more equal basis, sharing domestic chores and having more time for joint leisure activities. The more you can imagine the reality of these outcomes, the more they will lodge in your brain as incentives to make you commit to achieving your Aim. These positive thoughts are your 'Carrot' Commitments.

Now turn the situation around and ask yourself what you will lose if you don't achieve this Aim. Again, project yourself into the future and visualize the reality of your life. If your Work Aim is to organize your work so you can leave the office on time and spend an hour with your children at least three evenings a week, imagine a worst case scenario resulting from your failure to do this. Perhaps your partner has become disaffected with you and found other interests, or even another person, to fulfil their needs. Imagine your young children as teenagers, disillusioned with you valuing work time over time with them. Perhaps they have become rebellious and beyond your control; perhaps they have developed a negative take on everything you hold dear. Once more, imagine the reality of this scenario in detail – be specific. You can use this powerful memory in the future, when you feel tempted to give up on your Aim. This is one of your 'Stick' Commitments.

Remember, too, that whether you are reviewing the outcomes of a Work Aim or a Home Aim, it could affect both areas of your life.

Write down your Carrot and Stick Commitments on the form opposite, because you may need to use them to keep yourself on track from time to time.

If you find it helpful, write more about the Carrot and Stick images you have conjured up in your Balance Book, and refer back to them in the future.

Sarah

Sarah said that when she thought about what she would lose if they didn't sort out the work situation at Class Cleaners (her husband's health, time with her young grandchildren), it made her feel quite tearful. "And, if I'm honest, I realize we're also missing out on a decent home. I'm not sure whether Tom has really noticed, but our house is a mess. I don't have time to shop or cook proper meals and I am embarrassed if anyone drops round, to see the state we're living in."

Commitments

WORK AIM 1: _____
_____

If I achieve it I will gain:
-
-
-
-
-

If I don't achieve it I will lose:
-
-
-
-
-

HOME AIM 1: _____
_____

If I achieve it I will gain:
-
-
-
-

If I don't achieve it I will lose:
-
-
-
-
-

Sarah told Tom that things had gone beyond a joke and they couldn't sort it out on their own. Tom agreed to call a full staff meeting and tell them things had to change. Sarah and Tom asked if the staff had any suggestions about what would make them stay with Class Cleaners (given that wages couldn't rise), and how extra work could be covered. When the staff realized that Tom and Sarah were asking for their help and co-operation they began to come up with a whole range of suggestions. "We just hadn't realized what a diverse group of people they were and how they wanted to work outside the 9-5 limits we had stuck with. Amit wanted time off for religious festivals, Margaret had a sick husband who needed her to pop in at lunchtimes, Renée had to collect children from school and Ian wanted to train for his athletics competitions some mornings, but was happy to work a late shift on the machines."

Between them they worked out what hours the current staff could cover and what part-time extra help they needed to find. By then people were suggesting friends and relatives who could work lunch-times, a couple of hours here and there.

They didn't sort things out overnight, but within three months Tom and Sarah were working reasonable hours, and Sarah had hired a cleaner for the first time in her life. She was able to help her daughter by collecting her grandchildren from school a couple of days a week. "We're even thinking of taking a week's holiday soon. We haven't lost a single member of staff, but we've gained some part-time people who work odd hours, but to suit us and them. Sickness absence has more than halved and the atmosphere in the shop is great. We have a monthly schedule so we know who's off when, well in advance, and we cover the absences between us."

CHAPTER 5

Deciding on change and what to do next

THIS CHAPTER CONSIDERS:

- What kind of work do you really want?

- Your skills, abilities, attitudes and interests – abilities and interests, knowledge and skills, attitudes to the work experience, what sort of organization suits you best?

- Planning your next move – defining your goal, plotting your moves, skilling up, investment, financial planning, downshifting, calculating your timescale.

- Your plan of action and your timeframe.

- Finding the right employer – large and medium-sized employers, the job application process.

- How does your potential employer check out?

- Setting up on your own – define your offer, research your market, business plans, marketing and sales plans.

- Getting off to a flying start.

- Enacting your Aims.

You may have worked your way through some or all of the previous chapters, used the exercises to evaluate your position and decided as a result that you're either in the wrong job, working for the wrong manager or organization, or doing work that just doesn't suit you.

Then again, you may have known for some time that you want to make major changes to your working life. Equally, you may not currently have a job through choice, life-stage or redundancy, and want to use this opportunity to weigh up what kind of work and working lifestyle would suit you best. This chapter is where we look at the different issues you need to consider in order to make the right choices for your future, and how to build a practical plan of action to get you where you want to be.

What kind of work do you really want?

It's not an easy decision to make a major job or career change, and turning your ideas into a viable reality may well involve hard work and some sacrifices in the short term. But finding the work that you are best at, most suited to and most satisfied by will turn out to be a rewarding exercise, and one that is likely to bring you better balance in all areas of your life.

You may already have decided what your ideal new job or line of work is to be. However, if at this stage it's more a case of knowing what you want to get away from, but you are not completely clear about what you want to do next, here are some ways to help you focus on what might best suit you. In order to discover this you need to look at your innate abilities and interests, your experiential knowledge and skills, and your attitudes towards the most important aspects of the work experience.

Your skills, abilities, attitudes and interests

Abilities and interests

What are you good at and what do you enjoy? Two simple enough questions, perhaps with obvious answers, but when they're asked in relation to choosing a new career, you may need to give both considerably more thought. If your first response is 'nothing' or 'not much', make this exercise one in which you deliberately seek out all the talents you undoubtedly possess; use it to reinforce your belief in yourself and rid yourself of any negative self-image. Being able to use and develop as many of your natural abilities and interests as possible is perhaps the first criterion you should look for in a job or area of work.

Of course, it's possible that you may be very gifted at something you don't enjoy; it's still worth recognizing this skill and seeing whether it could be a useful additional selling point, even if you don't want to make it the main focus of your career. Also, ask yourself *why* you don't enjoy doing something you're good at; is it more to do with bad associations about when/how you've had to use this ability in the past than the actual activity itself?

Exercise

Look at the area headings and examples overleaf. Take your Balance Book and (under the six headings) list as many things as you can think of that you have enjoyed and been successful at in these environments.

Your abilities and interests

At home/in the family	Amongst friends/peer group	In the community
eg: Dealing with money Designing/decorating your home Caring for others (children or adults) Parenting Psychology Cooking Entertaining Organizing outings, holidays	eg: Co-ordinating travel plans Organizing events Listening Advising Entertaining Persuading Amusing Enthusing	eg: Campaigning Bringing people together Supporting others Organizing events Selling or advertising Fundraising Accounts
Education: school, college, university, training	**Work: for an employer, private work, personal research**	**Hobbies, leisure activities, interests, sports**
eg: Arts/science subjects Languages Calculations Reading Gathering information Writing Speaking in class Creative work Physical activities Manual dexterity Picking up ideas quickly Working methodically	eg: Organizing (offices, people) Creating systems Using IT Writing (reports, letters) Dealing with people Overcoming problems Carrying out directions Financial work (auditing, book-keeping) Creative work (writing, designing etc) Selling, presenting	eg: DIY Gardening Politics The arts Science The environment Squash, golf, tennis, football etc Walking, climbing Travel Fashion

When you've come up with as many abilities and interests as you can, check through the different areas and see if you can find any overlap or similarities. For example, do you enjoy managing your own finances, were you a good maths student? Have you enjoyed creating systems in the office or perhaps organized the finances of a local charity shop? Perhaps you did well at history in school because you enjoyed reading all the information and analyzing it for your essays, or perhaps you have been particularly good at researching and presenting information in various jobs, or perhaps you thrive on political discussions with your friends because you read the papers avidly and have the facts to back up your views. Were you good at art as a child, enjoy decorating your home, love to follow fashion and always make your work environment attractive?

If you can find one or more through-lines of aptitude and appeal in your life, try to summarize them into one overarching statement. For example, "I have a talent for seeking out and assimilating information and presenting it in a logical and accessible way". Or "I have a strongly developed visual sense and am talented in the area of visual design". If you have worked in a number of different jobs, look back through them and see if there is a particular talent you've successfully used in different activities or circumstances. For example, "I have always been able to create transparent and effective systems, whether in finance, office administration or personnel management." Whether or not you are able to pick out one or more of these underlying abilities from your previous experience, now go through your list and reduce it to three key talents that you enjoy, and would most like to use in your work.

Rob

Rob had never thought of himself as being good at anything. He may have been dyslexic because he found it hard to read books and concentrate on academic work. But he had always been good at sport, especially soccer, had played in school teams right through school, and still played for his local club. "I know I'm not good enough to be professional, but the thing is I do like kids. I always used to be the leader of a little gang when I was younger and the school soccer coach used to ask me to run training sessions if he was away". Rob was wondering whether there could be a career for him in sports training. He decided to use an internet search engine to look up 'sports coaching' careers, and said he would go back to his old school and ask the coach for advice. He also remembered there was a careers advisory service near his home and went to check it out.

Your knowledge and skills

Complementing your natural abilities and interests are the skills and knowledge that you have accumulated through your activities to date. The experiences through which you have acquired these competencies (as they are often called in the context of employment) are not necessarily work-related. In fact, these 'transferable skills' are as, if not more, likely to have been picked up through another aspect of your life. So, if you are currently looking for your first job, or feel that you want to make such a complete change that little or none of your previous experience will be relevant, this exercise is as much for you as anyone else. It is important for you to be aware and confident of your own knowledge and skills so can you describe and present them to a future employer or client.

Exercise

Take the six areas of the previous exercise and go through them again, this time looking for acquired knowledge and skills that you can bring to your new field of work or employer. Once again, you may have gained skills that you don't particularly enjoy using, in which case you don't want to make these the focus of your future work. They may, however, still be a useful adjunct to those you do enjoy.

Your knowledge and skills

At home/in the family	Amongst friends/peer group	In the community
eg: Financial management Conflict resolution Time management Property purchase/maintenance Childcare Eldercare Teaching Catering Leadership Creative techniques Empathetic skills Knowledge of work-life balance	eg: Teamwork Communication skills Events management Sales technique Facilitation (of meetings, discussions) Leadership Support skills	eg: Environmental/medical/educational knowledge Project management Sales technique Marketing Fundraising skills Events co-ordination Counselling skills Teaching Facilitation
Education: school, college, university, training	**Work: for an employer, private work, personal research**	**Hobbies, leisure activities, interests, sports**
eg: Arts/science knowledge Language skills Research techniques Report writing Presentation skills Design skills Self-motivated working Team working Self-discipline Remote-working skills IT skills, experience	eg: Organizational skills Systems development IT skills Report/letter writing Interpersonal communications Leadership Support skills Financial skills (auditing, book-keeping) Design, presentation of materials Sales, presentation Telephone skills Customer/client-facing skills Brainstorming techniques	eg: Motivational skills Construction, electrical, plumbing skills Gardening Knowledge of politics, arts, science etc Sports skills Team skills Knowledge of other countries, cultures

Again, it will be useful to look for through-lines of skills and knowledge development, eg your IT skills may have started at home, been developed at college, in other jobs and during your community work. If you are going to put together a new CV in which IT features, you will be able to list all the knowledge you have acquired of, for example, different systems and software, along with how you have been able to use it. Perhaps you feel you are being drawn to work which involves your interest in design; in which case decorating your own home(s) will have gained you valuable experience and skills, as will the advice you have given to friends and family on their homes.

Perhaps you take holiday photos and make them into attractive albums or collages, or maybe you were involved in the new design and layout of the office; all these activities have added to your fund of transferable knowledge and skills. You may be able to make money out of your ability to empathize and communicate with other people by becoming a mentor, coach or counsellor. Do friends and colleagues regularly come to you for guidance? Do your family trust your judgement and the safe-keeping of their confidences? Are you pleased when people say you are a good listener and they value your advice? Try to recall as many situations as you can when you've been able to help people through problems; think about what skills you used to do so.

While you want to maximize the spread and depth of your transferable skills (especially if you are writing a CV or brochure), it may be helpful for you to focus down on which skills you feel most confident with, enjoy using and want to develop further in your future work. So select the three main skills or knowledge-bases that you would like to feature in your new field of work or job.

Della

> Della had had what she called "this crazy idea of helping people to organize their lives and their homes better. I think it is a skill – lots of my friends tell me they'd like to be able to run their homes like I do and I have re-organized all the admin systems in the office. But it's not just systems, it's organizing a whole environment." Della's home was arranged to make life easier for her, and she had re-arranged her company's office layout so that everyone could communicate better and move around more easily. "The thing is, when I do that places do look good. The more I think about it, the more it seems that this is a service I could sell, if I could just explain it right to people. I wonder what they'd pay, though …"

Your attitudes towards the work experience

Having established the key abilities and skills you would like to exploit, enjoy and get paid for, we need to take a look at how, where and with whom you will work most productively. There is a wide range of options for you to consider; the most obvious are working as:

- a paid employee of an organization;

- a partner/director in an established business;

- an owner/director of your own business;

- a self-employed individual;

- a sole trader or formal/informal partnership;

- a consultant, working directly for clients and/or through a consultancy or agency.

The size, sector, structure and objectives of an employer organization are all aspects you will need to consider, but in general the basic benefits of becoming a member of staff include a regular pay packet, if not job security then a defined notice period, financial benefits such as paid leave, participation in an organizational pension scheme, some job-related training and often union or legislative access to redress in the case of unfair treatment. Of course, the greater your qualifications and experience the more extensive your pay packet, share in organizational success and access to further benefits. A medium-sized or large employer will also offer options for promotion and development, while a small employer may offer the environment and atmosphere of a 'family' firm with a sense of personal involvement in the organization's success.

An employer with good work-life balance policies and practices will offer flexibility of working patterns; sadly, however, even in best practice organizations individual managers can be inconsistent in their application of such policies. Check whether a prospective employer mentions flexibility or part-time working in their initial job advertisement and/or in the information sent to job applicants. Either way, ask about flexibility and work-life balance at your interview and, if your questions are met with a less than open or defensive response, be wary of accepting a position with such an organization. A small business may not have formal policies or processes in place, but may operate informal flexible working – though they may not recognize such terms as 'flexible working' or 'work-life balance'. Again, check at the interview stage whether you will be able to work in a way that suits you as well as meeting business needs, and whether managers are prepared to be flexible.

Working for yourself can appear to be a highly flexible option, but if you are setting up a new business you will probably find that the initial months or even years of building a steady flow of customers/clients/sales involve you in long hours and focused commitment. You do, however, have the ability to create your ideal team of people and implement your own flexible working policies and practices.

Operating as a consultant or partnership can provide the support of team working and the input of skills complementary to your own, while offering flexibility of time and place. On the other hand it lacks the security of being employed – a regular pay packet, guaranteed workflow, paid holidays etc.

Claire, managing a small business from home

"When working from home you can become engrossed and find it hard to break away from the job in hand to cook a meal for yourself or others. It takes a bit of discipline, and you need to put feelings of guilt aside; I have to remember that there is life besides work! I have become a bit better at this, but still find I work all hours. I am getting better at handling the guilt of not finishing everything immediately, or the feeling of wondering whether I am giving my all or not. Looking at others who just do a job, then go home and just live a life, helps. I think I care too much (which may or may not be a good thing), and I try to put work issues aside after hours.

"Luckily it hasn't affected my son at all, though he occasionally asks whether we can have dinner before 8:30pm!

"Working such long hours does add stress, and I find I really need quiet times to unwind. Somehow I don't seem to get these breaks, which adds more stress etc. Makes me wonder why I'm knocking my brains out… but there is that small thing called salary so I suppose I get on the best I can.

"Anyhow, positive things I have done are:

- I bought a new desk which is bigger and where I can spread my work, not using the floor as a desk extension.

- I quit at 6:30pm at the latest.

- I don't turn on the computer until after 8:30 in the morning. I try not to turn it on at all over weekends.

- I think about my alternatives (ie a different/another job); I know I have the final decision of whether I want to do this or not, and while the answer is Yes I tell myself to stop moaning.

- If a project is not finished, or is not perfect, well, I did the best I could.

"I suspect this is similar to everyone else on the planet, but hope it helps a little."

Becoming a sole trader can offer maximum flexibility, and working from home gives you the chance to integrate your work and home activities with minimum restriction; but the self-discipline and comparative isolation involved is not for everybody. People who enjoy the structured environment of a workplace and associated sociability need not apply. If, however, your preferences are to set your own objectives and working arrangements, and integrate your work and personal lives, then this scenario could be ideal. Remember, you will need to take on other aspects of running your own business such as finance and administrative responsibilities, marketing and project planning.

Exercise

You may already have experience of one or more of these situations (and know which suits you best), but if you are uncertain complete the following quick exercise to give yourself some pointers.

What sort of work organization suits you best?

Look at the seven headings below. Now circle the one option under each heading that best describes your attitude towards it.

WORKING STYLE
A I like clear instructions and a defined task
B I like work to be defined and allocated by the team
C I like to set my own goals and work in my own way
MANAGEMENT
A I like to work with a strong leader
B I like to share responsibility with equals
C I like to be my own boss
COLLEAGUES
A I like to have a defined role in relation to others
B I like everyone in the team to be equally respected
C I like to work on my own
SETTING
A I like a well-appointed workplace with good facilities
B I like a comfortable workplace where I feel at home
C I don't mind where I work as long as I can set my own agenda
ENVIRONMENT
A I like to feel part of a large organization
B I like to be part of a bonded team
C I like working on my own or with a few chosen others

WORK PATTERNS
A I like to stick to regular working hours and days
B I value flexibility for myself, but am happy to be flexible in return
C I like to be completely flexible and unrestricted in organizing my work
WORK-LIFE BALANCE
A I like clear policies at work about flexible work arrangements and leave
B I like to know I can take leave or time off when I need it
C I like to balance home and work according to changing needs

Mostly As: You are best suited to working for a large organization where there are well-defined ways of operating. Your life outside work may be highly demanding at present, and you will be most comfortable with clear-cut working arrangements and the support and structure that a large private or public sector organization can offer. However, you may also be able to find this environment in well-organized medium-sized or small organizations. Working for yourself or as a consultant is unlikely to suit you in your present life-stage as you prefer to operate in an environment that is defined by others rather than setting your own goals.

Equal As & Bs: You will also be most comfortable working within an organization, but you could find your ideal employer is either a large or a smaller business. A well-organized small or medium-sized employer could provide the egalitarian structure you like to work in, but so could a team-based position in a larger corporation. Self-employment or consultancy work is unlikely to suit you, unless it is in the context of a close-knit, structured team.

Mostly Bs: You enjoy working in a team environment where work allocation, working patterns and cover is organized in a collegiate way, taking account of everyone's needs in relation to business objectives. As you prefer equality among colleagues rather than a hierarchical structure, you would probably find team-working within a large or medium-sized organization as satisfactory as being a partner or director in a shared business. You might enjoy consultancy work if it involved collaboration with others, but self-employment or working as a sole trader is too solitary a style for you.

Equal Bs and Cs: You prefer a self-motivated and self-determined working style, but also enjoy some team-based activity. You could find your ideal role within an organization if it allowed you to do project work or research on your own for at least some of the time. Equally, you could deal with self-employment, running your own small business or consultancy, if it involved some interaction with others, perhaps working closely with clients. You might find home-working somewhat restricting and isolating and might prefer working from another base where you had regular contact with others.

Mostly Cs: You are an ideal candidate for setting up your own business, either on your own or working with a small number of colleagues. You are self-motivated, self-disciplined and prefer not to be restricted in your working arrangements. Consultancy work, creative work, providing professional or skilled services is probably what you enjoy and, given strong marketing, you could find this a very satisfactory way of making a living. You would prefer to be either based at home or be able to carry out a lot of your work at home, as this gives you the flexibility to organize your work around your (perhaps changing) personal requirements.

Mostly As and Cs, or equal As, Bs and Cs: You have a complex set of working preferences, some of which may appear contradictory. If you have high levels of skills and experience in a particular field you might find that becoming a partner in an existing firm which specializes in this area could suit your requirements. Alternatively, you might be able to combine, for example, a part-time job within a large organization with some consulting work, or work on a permanent consultancy basis to an established business.

Ed

> Ed felt he was suited to working on his own, or with a loose group of colleagues. He scored 100% Cs, which made him even more certain that it was time to start his own business. He thought he could get going on his own, but could also identify a group of freelancers who could give him back-up in specialist areas and would be interested in odd bits of work here and there. "Although I don't spend much time in the office in my present job, and I'm called a 'consultant', I am still an employee and I have to dance to the company tune, which gets on my nerves a lot of the time. I could offer clients much more creative solutions if I wasn't restricted to company product."

Exercise

To get an overview of the kinds of work you would find most satisfying, and are most suited to, and the working structure and environment in which you would flourish, fill in the following form.

The parameters of your ideal work

ABILITIES AND INTERESTS	
The three key abilities and interests I want to focus on in my next job/new career are:	1.. .... 2.. .... 3.. ....
KNOWLEDGE AND SKILLS	
The three main areas of knowledge and skills I want to make use of in my next job/new career are:	1.. .... 2.. .... 3.. ....
WORKING ENVIRONMENT	
Either: I plan to look for work with:	....
Or: I plan to set up my own:	....

Extended exercise

If this doesn't provide you with enough information about where you are heading, go back to Chapter 3 or your Balance Book and revisit the bumper checklist with its summary of your values and needs. Put these alongside the last checklist summarizing your abilities, interests, knowledge and skills, and spend some time thinking, or writing in your Balance Book, about where this combination of requirements might take you.

For example, if one of your key needs was to be useful, one of your values was to contribute, and your ideal working environment is a small or medium-sized organization, you might consider looking for jobs in a range of voluntary sector organizations. There are charities large and small which support arts, cultural and scientific causes, social issues and individuals and groups with all kinds of needs, and which employ variously skilled and experienced personnel.

You might have identified your preference for working in a large organization, have needs around gaining and winning and values involving leadership and influencing. Whatever your current position or experience, consider how you would get a job at a major organiza-tion whose business coincides with your abilities and skills, and picture yourself working your way up to the senior management team, perhaps even CEO.

Again, your needs may indicate calm and order, your values comprise enlightening others and a desire for spirituality, you would like to work for yourself and enjoy your yoga classes. Even if your work to date has been in the accounts department of a multinational company, how long would it take you to train as a yoga teacher, offer your services either publicly or privately and slowly build up an individual or shared practice?

Allow yourself time for your brain to do some lateral thinking, both consciously and subconsciously, while you are involved in other activities. Don't dismiss any idea your mind throws up, no matter how impossible it may seem. It might have at least the germ of your future within it. Allow yourself to remain open to as many options as present themselves until either one takes the lead position in your mind or contacts, circumstances or information lead you (apparently co-incidentally) down a particular path.

Renata, running her own jewellery company and studying

"Being single means I don't have as many problems as most, but I am also doing an MA part time at the moment and the further I get into the course the harder it is to not spend the time on the projects that I find really interesting, and hope will help me out a lot in the future. I sometimes find it hard to have time to visit my parents and friends; and it's not just the time, it's also the money, working for myself with no guaranteed income each week is difficult. One bonus, though, is that I have a special event every year that most of my friends and family are invited to, and they all seem to love coming.

"Money is always a problem and the longer I run my company, and the more I commit to (such as higher rents and other extra overheads), the harder it is if I do have a bad month. I have always kept my head above water and paid the bills on time, but I go without a lot to keep my business going, and am probably paid lower than the minimum wage all year round let alone quiet times of year. Exhaustion doesn't seem to be a problem, I love doing my MA and my business and I am pretty happy much of the time.

"I think anyone who starts a business is brave and dedicated, and anyone that starts one as a jewellery designer/maker is even more so. If anyone is not overworked and underpaid to start with I would be very surprised. My business has changed a lot over the years, growing and developing. I am now putting more changes into action mainly due to a lot of customers' companies closing down and not paying for the work I have done for them. I have had to find the right balance between designing and making. As a maker it can be hard to charge a decent amount for your work and I have decided to do a lot more design work as well as continuing with the designing/making side of things.

"Most jewellers work on a sale or return basis to shops. If I cut down the sale or return work I will need to cover the loss of sales somehow. I plan to do this by expanding the product design side of the business, where work is more appreciated and normally paid for immediately. Other changes since starting the business have been steady growth and a move into retail; this has all worked well with the original business plan and I hope to continue at a steady pace."

Planning your next move

Making a major life change in terms of your job or career is not something that needs to be a total leap in the dark. Now you have some idea of where you are going, a well-planned series of steps towards achieving your goal will provide a framework for action. The first step must be to define an ultimate goal to achieve over a particular period of time. You can develop this goal and move it forward when required, but having an end-point in sight to work towards is crucial to your plan.

Defining your goal

Having worked through the exercises above you should now have some idea of what area of work you would like to be in and the kinds of working arrangements that would suit you best. You may be someone who knows quite precisely where they would like to be when they have achieved their goal, in which case your definition might read: "I will join a legal practice which focuses on family casework and become a senior specialist in divorce."

You may not have defined your aims so specifically, but should still be able to formulate your goal as it currently stands. For example: "I will make a career in design and plan to find a group of designers with complementary skills who want to work creatively together."

It may be that you are more sure of the working environment (or even the geographical location) that you are drawn to than the specific area of work you want to be in, which is also an appropriate way of defining your goal: "I will get a job in a major, multinational organization and will consider any positions that involve technology and travel" or "I will move to a rural location, within half an hour's drive to the nearest city, and run a mail order business from home."

In your Balance Book, head a new page 'Plan of Action' and, at the *bottom* of the page, write out your goal.

Plotting your moves

At the top of the page, write a similar description of where you are now, in terms of work. You can be quite specific about this, whether it's something like "I am a level 2 support operative in the IT department of (a large retail company)" or "I am in my last year at college, working part-time in a bar until I graduate in six months."

Your next step is to fill in the page between your current position and your goal with the specific steps it will take to move from one point to the other.

Caroline, magazine editor and parent

"Since we returned from living overseas my husband (who works in oil) has never been able to live at home during the week. His job has taken him up and down the country and we cannot disrupt the children. So, during the week I am a single parent. It's tough. I work as a freelance journalist and editor and frequently travel to conferences all over the world. Our kids are 8 and 10 and I try hard to be here during term time, and unless I have to be away, work from 9.00-3.30pm only. It is tough with an office in the house, but I do stick to working during the week and always stop working at supper time.

"A long time ago I decided to employ a cleaner and this has made a huge difference. Jenny does the washing and ironing, which is great. I feel that the balance is about right. In the holidays I work the minimum, about three hours a day. In term time I regularly do six hours. It is when I go away that I feel the guilt, especially as something always seems to go wrong at home.

"For the most part it works. I decided that time was often worth more than money, and I work freelance so that I can fit around the children. I also made a conscious decision to work out which elements of my portfolio of work earned me the most money in the shortest time, and stick to those. I rarely turn work down, but often price myself highly rather than say No. At least it is worth my while when I do choose to do extra work.

"One thing that has made a huge difference is that my parents live two miles away. It is amazing how much easier it is to leave children with those you know love them. It is also much easier to ask for help myself, I find.

"My biggest problem is 'me time'. I resent paying for a babysitter so I can go out in the evening. Day time is work time and I rarely, if ever, allow myself to window shop, go for lunch, visit a gym or watch day-time TV. By the evening I am too tired to do anything constructive with my time.

"I still feel that I made the right choice, and with my husband away so much this is about the best arrangement for the whole family."

Skilling up

Take a minute to revisit the 'Knowledge and skills' list you created in your Balance Book and evaluate whether you have all, some, or any of the qualifications or skills required to attain your goal; whether your knowledge and skills relate to the content or style of the work you are aiming for. If not, where can you acquire these skills? By taking a course, through self-learning, through experience such as volunteering or an internship? Perhaps you will have to spend time gaining experience in another job before you are able to apply for the one in your goal. If you need to gain skills or experience do some research about how best you can achieve them: call companies and ask what their requirements are; talk to people you know in that line of work; use the internet to find out about organizations, courses, professional bodies and support groups. However much unexpected work you discover is involved, don't be put off reaching your goal. Write down the results of your research in your Balance Book, and what you will have to do.

Investment

What costs are you going to incur in up-grading your skills? If you have to take a course, find out what the fees will be. If you have to take time off from your current job, how much money will you lose? Will it help you to join a professional organization? If so, calculate the cost of membership and ask if there are concessions for trainees or a cheaper associate membership rate. Books, publications, software, CDs and other sources of information need to be budgeted for, but your local library may be able to help, as may friends and contacts willing to lend or pass on materials to you. You may need to buy yourself other work-related equipment, which could be anything from a car or computer to a work bench or mobile phone.

You will probably need to update and print out copies of your CV, perhaps produce business cards, a portfolio of previous work, a website or other marketing materials in order to sell yourself or your product. (We'll give you more specific tips about setting up your own business later in this chapter.) Shop around for inexpensive ways to create these materials, but don't undersell yourself by looking tacky. Calculate what all this is going to cost. You may need new clothes to wear to job interviews or networking meetings – it's a worthwhile investment to create the right image for potential employers, clients or customers. Again, do some bargain hunting but not at the risk of looking cheap. When you've produced what seems to you like an exhaustive list of everything you need, list them on your Plan of Action page in your Balance Book, with the maximum cost for each item.

Financial planning

You may be able to accomplish some or all of what it will take to achieve your goal while you are still in your current job – during evenings and weekends, or by taking some unpaid or holiday leave. Or you may need to have an employment break while you do training, attend college or set up a business or home office. Your financial and other needs must still be met, so revisit the exercises in Chapter 3 and your basic material needs. Work out how you can continue to cover these during any period you are not earning, or bringing in less money than covers your expenses. Options might include taking out a loan from your bank (or a relative or friend with some excess cash), extending your mortgage, cashing in an insurance policy or digging into your savings. Don't approach any of these without having a written plan of exactly how much you will need for what period of time, what your expenses will be during this period, and when and how the money will be repaid (even into your own savings account). Alternatively, you may be able to take a temporary job with hours which fit around your other commitments, sell a valuable item like a car, rely on a partner's income or reduce your outgoings temporarily.

Downshifting

It's not unusual for people making a job or career change to look to a reduced income for a fixed or indefinite period of time. If you have been earning well while working in a stressful job or environment, you may be looking at re-prioritizing aspects of your life. You may be willing to trade your material gains for better quality of life in terms of relationships and time with your partner, family and friends. There is a growing trend for couples and families in their 30s and 40s to move out of cities to live in more rural surroundings where the pace of life is slower. A move such as this might allow you to buy a similar-sized or larger house for the same or less money than your town house, with lower running costs. The expensive status symbols of the rat-race – cars, clothes, possessions and lifestyle – may start to lose their appeal as you consider a new working life where fulfilling your needs and values seems a more worthwhile reward than the level of your salary.

If downshifting is a route that appeals to you, make very careful financial plans. Research the costs of, for example, changed accommodation and the travel involved in being in a different location. If you are considering doing without a second, or any, car, how much will you need to spend on public transport and cabs; is it really less? To sum up, don't make any moves without first discussing them with other people involved – your partner, children, extended family or new business colleagues. Their agreement to, and support for, your new lifestyle will be crucial. Their needs and values will hopefully be aligned to your own, but you won't achieve better balance in your lives if you try to fulfil your needs at the expense of other people's.

If downshifting is part of your changed work plans, you will need to be very clear about your financial planning. Go back to the financial exercises in Chapter 3 and re-work them around your revised proposition. Make sure that you can really live at the level you are suggesting and that your reduction in income will not cause significant imbalance or genuine discomfort in other areas of your life. It is true, though, that many people who change jobs to something which gives them greater personal satisfaction end up earning more money than they expected – perhaps because of their greater enthusiasm or aptitude for their new work.

Add your financial plans to the lists of steps in your Balance Book for moving you from your current position to your goal.

Calculating your timescale

Now you have defined your goal and determined the steps that will move you towards it, you can formulate a timetable for achieving it.

Take each individual action or step that you have listed, from going on a course to speaking with your mortgage-lender to re-organize payments. Allocate to each step a realistic amount of time, not only to complete the step itself (eg the length of the course) but also to set it up (eg to research, access and enrol). Make sure that you have included informal steps, such as having a conversation with your partner about your new plans and allowing them time to think about and challenge you on some (or all!) of them. Then arrange your steps in the order you will carry them out (some will have over-lapping timeframes) and work out how long it will take you to achieve your goal. Within the overall framework, build in some 'milestones' at which you can take stock and celebrate your progress – for example, when you have completed some training, given in notice on your current job, bought your new equipment or put together your team. Now take a fresh page in your Balance Book (or use the form on p. 178) and set these steps out on a 'monthly calendar' for the period you have planned to achieve your goal. Note, also, any key dates you have set yourself and try to keep to them as closely as possible. If something does slip, readjust your timescale so you are still working towards a realistic deadline. If you find that you are consistently not meeting your own deadlines or achieving the steps towards your goal, ask yourself *why*. Are your timescales unrealistic? Have unexpected obstacles surfaced that need to be taken into account? Are they surmountable – or not? Have you set yourself the wrong goal and do you need to rethink where you are going?

Naomi and Ed

Naomi and Ed discussed their future plans in more detail and finally agreed that Ed should make a move as quickly as possible, and that then, if things were settling down, they would start trying for a family. Ideally, they would then both cut down on work and share the childcare. But if Ed's business wasn't working out as well as he planned, Ed would do more with the baby while Naomi maintained their income. "That's fair," said Ed, "because financially she's going to support me while I give up work and set up the new business. And she's allowing a certain amount of our joint savings to finance the start up, so I really feel supported by her, but also I've got to do my utmost to make it work."

They planned a slight downshifting for about six months – not moving house, cutting down on personal expenditure, getting rid of both their expensive cars and buying a couple of smaller, cheaper-to-run models. Then Naomi's income would cover Ed for three months while he put the business together and their savings would go into his equipment and building an extension for a home office. Naomi said she would "give it a year in total – three months set up and nine months to bed in – to meet certain financial returns. If it hasn't, then Ed has to look around for a job more locally and with less travel". They agreed it was a somewhat scary, but exciting, step for them both.

Exercise

Your plan of action

If you can fill in the following form, your action plan is in good shape.

My current position is:	....
My financial investment will be:	1 .... £/$..................... 2 .... £/$..................... 3 .... £/$..................... 4 .... £/$..................... Total: £/$.....................
The key skills I need to acquire are:	1 .... 2 .... 3 ....
The key people I need to consult/gain agreement from are:	1 .... 2 .... 3 ....
The financial steps I need to take are:	1 .... 2 .... 3 ....
My overall timescale is: With the following milestones at:	From: ..../........./........... To: ..../........../....... 1 .... At: ..../......./....... 2 .... At: ..../......./....... 3 .... At: ..../......./.......
My goal is:	....

Your timeframe

Fill in your moves, highlighting milestones towards your goal.

	Skills	Finance	People	Equip-ment	Organi-zational	Other
Month 1						
Month 2						
Month 3						
Month 4						
Month 5						
Month 6						
Month 7						
Month 8						
Month 9						
Month 10						
Month 11						
Month 12						
Month 13						
etc						

Finding the right employer

You've done some exercises around the sort of working environment that would best suit you in your new or re-organized line of work. You may have decided that you will be happiest and most fulfilled by working as an employee of a business. Benefits such as being part of an organization with the right environment and equipment, having a guaranteed pay and benefits package, a career structure, a defined role and the support of others around you are substantial reasons for working in this way. Nonetheless, there can be downsides, such as inflexible hierarchies and working practices, lack of influence and working with uncongenial managers and colleagues. It's important to check out both sides of the equation and see how they balance up before deciding to take up a job with any employer. Equally, if you are searching more widely for a range of organizations you might want to work for, here are some tips on checking them out.

Large and medium-sized employers

It is a rare company these days that does not have its own website, so this is likely to be the first access point in your research. Look for their value or mission statement as well as their areas of business and see whether it accords with your own needs and values. Where appropriate, look at their client or customer list and check whether these organizations are ones that you feel in sympathy with. Websites of employers with a good awareness of work-life balance are likely to carry information on their equal opportunities or diversity policies, environmental and community awareness, their training and education practices, and any non-profit schemes which they sponsor. If you want more information on, say, flexible working options, contact the HR department and ask them to send you a summary of their work-life balance or flexible working policies. Be wary of any large organization which says they don't operate flexible working arrangements, don't have any written policies or take each case on its merits. These could all indicate a lack of awareness about (or lack of respect for) employees' lives outside work.

A legally constituted business of any size will have to submit annual financial records and these are available to public scrutiny. In the UK, this information is lodged at Companies House. If you want more information about a large business in the private sector, newspaper websites are a good place to look. Use their internal archive search engines for stories about your potential employer and check to see whether they involve poor treatment of employees or activities which are not compatible with your own values. In any case, this sort of research may come in useful at a job interview where you are likely to be asked what you know about the company – a 'nothing' or 'not much' response is unlikely to impress.

The same goes for public sector employers (such as national or local government departments, public hospitals or education establish-ments), but you may also be able to access information about their organizational performance from professional bodies to which they belong and government departments to which they are accountable. Local sources such as libraries, local papers or radio stations could also provide you with useful information on public sector organizations as well as on smaller businesses and voluntary sector employers.

Dave and Karen

Dave and Karen had had their first "reasonable" discussion for months. After coming home early and helping to put the children to bed, Dave asked Karen if she would help him write a proposal to his boss to go on a training course. He explained that with a new qualification he could be promoted and earn more in shorter hours. He even said sorry for the way he'd been lately and allayed Karen's fears about an affair.

Karen said working together on the proposal had made her think about what she would really want out of a job, and that it was *not* the stress and the hours she used to have in catering. She decided on an ideal situation for her current life – working for a large organization on part-time hours that fitted in with the kids, decent pay and benefits and some nice people to work with. "So then I thought, what could I get that would give me all that around here, and I went and walked up and down the high street. There were two places I fancied, a major national retail chain and a major supermarket. I preferred the retailers, but rang them both anyway and asked what they had to offer; they both sent application forms." Neither had a problem offering part-time hours, but the pay was better at the retailers and Karen liked what they said about looking after their employees and the training she could access. She was now working there three mornings a week, with the option to extend her days and hours when Kylie started full-time school. "It feels great to be getting out of the house and earning some money, and the girls I'm working with are lovely – we have a real laugh and they've made it really easy to fit in. I wish I'd done it before. I'm helping to pay off our debts and so things are better between me and Dave too. I just hope he gets his training course."

The job application process

The earlier that flexible working options are indicated in the job-seeking process, the more confident you can be that an employer has a good understanding of employees' needs to balance their work and home lives. Best practice organizations with a strong grasp on how they can use flexibility to attract a diverse pool of recruits may mention flexible working options or work-life balance when advertising positions. Some even indicate that all jobs are open to part-time working. If this is not the case, though, look carefully at the material you are sent with your application form about terms and conditions of employment. No indication of flexible working practices at this point should prompt you to ask specifically about this issue if you take your application further.

A job interview is a crucial time to establish a potential employer's line on work-life balance. If it is not already clear, you should ask a question about flexible working policies. Even if you don't intend to making use of such arrangements immediately, you may well do in the future. If you have specific ideas about how your potential job could be carried out, for example working at home for part of the week, or on a job-share basis, raise this at your first interview. Take note of any reluctance to discuss the matter, or to dismiss such options as inappropriate to your job. Revisit Chapter 4 and our tips for putting forward a proposal for changed working arrangements to a manager. Think through some of the issues raised there before your interview.

Unfortunately, there are a number of employers, both large and small and in all market sectors, who may have a good set of written policies about flexible working but do not support managers in implementing them. As one major retailer said, "When people go they're not usually quitting the firm, but an unsatisfactory line manager".

Your potential line manager should be present at your job interview and his or her response to questions about flexibility are crucial to your future balance. If you get the chance, ask how many people in the team are currently working non-standard hours, or are able to work from home, and how such arrangements are organized. The ideal response would be that flexible options are open to everyone and that the practical arrangements are a balance between business/service needs and the personal needs of team members. If there is any discussion about how flexible work options can best be made to work, it may be in your interests to emphasize that you believe it is the joint responsibility of team members and managers to do this.

Tom and Sarah

> Tom and Sarah discovered that, as an employer, it made good sense to talk about flexibility from the start. "Before we started being more flexible we always said No to people who came in or wrote in asking for jobs working odd hours; I don't suppose it did our standing in the local community much good to seem so stick-in-the-mud" said Tom. Now Tom and Sarah found they hardly needed to advertise as friends and relatives of staff would ask if they could work at Class Cleaners, and if the hours they were offering were of use to the business they would take them on. They also offered flexible hours in a recruitment ad for drivers for a new collection and delivery service, and had far more applicants than ever before. Sarah commented: "The two people we picked, a man and a woman, work out the hours between them and they've never let us down yet. We're not paying them anything special, but it means a lot to them to be working around their home commitments."

Exercise

How does your potential employer check out on work-life balance?

When looking for a potential employer, or considering taking up a job with an organization, check their credentials for work-life balance against the following items (see overleaf).

	POSITIVE	NEUTRAL	NEGATIVE
Personal request for information (phone call/ letter/e-mail)			
Employer's website (including vision, employees, clients/customers, links)			
Public records (financial, legal)			
Other accountable/review bodies (eg government departments, regulatory bodies)			
Personal contacts (eg current or past employees)			
Job advertisements (flexible working options mentioned?)			
Application information (information about working practices included?)			
Job interview (response to subject of work-life balance/flexible working?)			
Induction materials (policies, practices relating to work-life balance/flexible options)			
TOTALS:			

Think carefully about whether you will be able to maintain a balanced life while working for any organization which clocks up more than a couple of 'Negatives' or less than six 'Positives'.

Setting up on your own

Whether you feel you are best suited to offering your services to organizations or individuals as a freelancer or a consultant, or whether this may be a stepping stone towards your ultimate goal of running your own business, the first steps are the same.

Define your offer

Having worked on the exercises earlier in this chapter around your abilities, skills, knowledge and the goal you want to achieve, the first step is to clarify what you are offering to your clients or customers. An easy mistake to make is to offer too much at first and confuse both yourself and your market about what you can do for them. Focus, in the first instance, on a limited area which you are *certain* you (and your associates if you have colleagues with you in this enterprise) can deliver. You can always expand your services later, but to start with concentrate on your most saleable and deliverable product. Identify what is different about your product or service – what is its 'Unique Selling Point' (USP)? Is it more efficient, cheaper or cost effective than the competition? Does it have special features which would attract certain groups of buyers?

Most importantly, assess your offer in terms of your ability to deliver it and still maintain balance in your life. Are you suggesting, even implicitly, to clients or customers that you will be available to them at all times, perhaps because you are working from home? If you are lucky enough to get a high take-up of your service, can you schedule work around your personal life, turn down excessive work or access colleagues you could share it with? Is your product a seasonal one? If so, have you considered how you will balance your life around the peaks and troughs of demand? Setting some initial ground rules about the boundaries between your working time and personal time is a valuable exercise to do *before* starting to work at home or in your own enterprise.

Write yourself a sales flyer: in your Balance Book compose a paragraph summarizing your product or service, add an eye-catching headline, then stand back and imagine how you would react if this came through your mailbox.

Jan, changing direction to find better balance

"Following a long and successful career with a large American pharmaceutical company, I decided, in my early 50s, to change career direction. 'You must be mad' said friends and colleagues, as they heard me plan to forfeit valuable pensionable years by resigning without the cushion of a redundancy payout. (My employer had no intention of making me redundant, because I wasn't. They had several alternative job opportunities, and valued my contribution to their business. I still see the look of disbelief on strangers' faces – 'she must have been sacked then' – not true at all.)

"So why did I do it? I wanted to balance my life, and to me – a single (divorced) person without children – that meant taking control over how I spent most of my waking hours. I wanted to work when/where/how I wanted to work, with the people and organizations I chose on subjects of personal interest. I definitely wanted to work, but I no longer wanted to work as dictated by others. Psychiatrist Professor Anthony Clare once said that stress was caused when individuals lost control – and that was how it was becoming for me.

"So what happened? First, I was fortunate that my employer retained me (and still does over three years later) as a consultant on the subjects of most interest to me, and where my expertise is still of most value to them.

Secondly, I was fortunate through contacts to become part of a major consultancy which taught me the ropes of self-employment, and helped me with the transition from big corporate team to small groups of like-minded working colleagues. I have now broken away from them, but their early support was invaluable.

"Is my life more balanced? Yes. I had idly thought that I would spend more time on the tennis court, but this I have not achieved. I find myself working virtually every day of the week to a greater or lesser extent, and taking holidays (again another imagined benefit) is much less frequent than before. Why? Because I don't feel the need.

"But I *do* have the control I sought. I only do the work that interests me – and fortunately there is plenty of that. Usually I am able to plan my time to suit the rest of my life. (Over the last six months I have had a major refurbishment of my house, which my flexible work schedule has facilitated.) It has sometimes meant that weekends merge into weekdays, but then weekdays can become weekends just as easily.

"To me, work-life balance is being able to juggle the priorities of your life in a way that causes maximum satisfaction and minimum stress. Those priorities could be caring for a dependant, pursuing your interests or, as for me, working on subjects of my choosing. This I have achieved, so for me life is entirely balanced. The next step is to spend more time on the tennis court, but, frankly, I am too busy enjoying working! When that stops, then so do I."

Research your market

Although you may be convinced that there is a demand for what you are offering, it's best to do some research and be certain. Define for yourself who or what you see as your core market – perhaps you had some of these in mind when you wrote the flyer for your product in your Balance Book. How are you going to reach at least a proportion of this market in order to research it? If your market is local, perhaps you could hand deliver some flyers or make appointments to visit some key potential customers. If you are aiming at a wider market, perhaps national or even international, either mail, telephone, e-mail or a combination of these could work well. How do you measure up against the competition?

Consider whether your choice of market is compatible with your personal life. Will it involve much travel and time away from home? Clients or customers operating in a different time zone may want to contact you while you and others in your household are asleep. If you plan to work locally to your home, will customers assume that they can call round to discuss business with you during the evening or weekends? If any of these downsides are possible, how will you prevent work impinging unnecessarily on other aspects of your life?

Having written an overview of your product/service in the form of a flyer, you might now want to expand on what you can offer a client with three or four additional bullet points. If your service is based on your personal skills, a few lines about your background and qualifications would be appropriate. Then, finally, you will need to put a price, or range of prices, on what you are offering. To do this calculate your own costs in providing/producing your product (including overheads such as your own office and administration, travel, marketing etc) and add as high a profit margin as you think the market will bear. This is as much as you will need to do your initial market research.

The next step is to write a personal message (probably in the form of a covering letter) to your potential customer, telling them you are starting up in business and asking if they would take five minutes to help you refine your service to suit their needs. Ask them to reply to the following (or similar) questions:

- Would you be interested in the service/product outlined?

- If so, under what circumstances?

- If not, what, if anything, would make you interested?

- Do you think the suggested price(s) is cheap/reasonable/excessive?

- How much/how often would you purchase the product/service?

- Is there anyone else you know who you think would be interested in this product/service?

- Please give any other comments as to how we might improve the service/product for you/your organization?

With this covering letter, product description and survey questionnaire, you have just devised your own set of market research tools. These can be used as the basis for a telephone script, a mailshot or an e-mail drop to your potential customers. Using these materials contact as wide a sample of your potential market as you can afford or think necessary, perhaps offering in your covering letter a start-up discount to those who return your questionnaire in order to generate a higher response. Don't forget to make use of people you already know who fit your client profile (ask for additional input and advice) as well as researching appropriate names and contact numbers/addresses of a wider market.

Working from home, or in your own business, can give you the flexibility to network with people at more convenient times, and in a greater range of situations, than traditional work hours. It is important, though, to bear in mind your own boundaries, and those of your partner or family, when it comes to networking; it can just become a round of aimless socializing.

When you've received sufficient responses to give you a feel for the market, analyze the results and consider adjusting your product, service and prices to appeal more specifically to potential clients. A follow-up marketing device would be to re-contact all your sample customers to tell them of the encouraging results and how you have, for example, reduced your prices in the first instance, or refined your product to be more appealing. Don't do this, though, until you have a start date for your new business.

Della

Della had decided to aim her new service at women like herself in the first place, because she knew the market and thought some friends might give her a go – or have other friends who might be interested. She called herself the 'Home Organizer' – and said her services were about saving time, money and stress and ranged from re-organizing household admin systems to redesigning kitchens. "I asked a couple of my friends if I could do something for them for free, if they would give me references – so I did that and added some quotes from them to my sales pitch. Then I hand-mailed my flyer with the little questionnaire to all the houses in three streets round here, where I know some of my potential clients live, and the office allowed me to hand some out to some of their clients."

Della was amazed at how many responses she received and pleased with some good suggestions for other services she could offer. She also got an idea of what people would pay. "So far I've had six clients. I've spent an average of two days with each of them and they've paid very reasonably.

They've all said they know other people who would be interested so I think I could be going to resign from my other job."

Business plans

Before you go ahead with your start-up date, do the essential financial groundwork and draw up a budget and a cash flow forecast. If this is something new, you can get advice, guidelines and even free software from your bank. You will certainly have to do this if you plan to borrow money for your start-up, and if this is the case the positive results of your market research should provide convincing support for your business plan. Even if you have the resources to finance your move to self-employment (or enough savings to put into starting up your own business venture), and even if you can win some business straightaway, remember it could be weeks or even months before your first invoices get paid.

Under-financing the start-up of your own business can cause severe problems for balanced living. If you have a partner their support is essential; drawing more deeply than planned on joint savings, or running up debts because of poor planning, is more than likely to cause problems and reduce support for you. If you and your partner are working together in the new enterprise it is important to define your roles in advance, stick to agreements about contribution and working hours, and to anticipate and make contingency plans for problems as far as possible in advance.

Make sure that, in addition to your bank, you have good professional advisors. You will certainly need an accountant, and if your turnover is high or your income and expenditure complex, you may need a book-keeper as well. They should be able to help you set up systems and records like credit and invoicing procedures, trading terms and conditions, and model contracts. Personal recommendations of such people from friends or business contacts can be valuable, and you might be able to offer work to other freelancers like yourself.

If you are starting up a business you will also need to have an efficient lawyer on board to keep your company records up to date and legal. It might be useful to consult a financial planning advisor at least once to talk about insurance, such as office contents and vehicle, pensions, medical and sickness cover and professional liability. Don't forget to talk to your tax office about your new position and responsibilities, and how they might affect your partner and family.

Naomi

As Ed was going to be working from their home, and perhaps with other people if business went well, Naomi wanted to be sure that he had gone through all the right (legally required) safety procedures and had proper insurance in setting up a home office. Their bank was helpful on some of these issues as well as the financial planning aspects. "It may have added to our costs a little, but I wanted to be sure that there was some insurance in case Ed fell ill, insurance to cover other people's health and safety if they were working in the home office, the right kind of wiring for the computers and full cover for replacement cost of the equipment."

Building the extension to their home was a lot of work and very disruptive, so Naomi left Ed to get on with supervizing it and took some time off to visit her sick mother back home. "My mum was so happy to hear we were planning to start a family, and I think it's given her something to look forward to. She was actually quite a lot better by the time I left, so I've come back to work much less stressed and all the more focused for having had a break."

Marketing and sales plans

You will have received some feedback on your initial sales pitch from your market research and, no matter how much work may be coming in at any one time, you will need to maintain an ongoing marketing strategy. In the first instance, make sure you have chosen an appropriate name for your service or business; check out what company and website names are legally available before publicizing a trading name which may already have been taken.

Communication is at the heart of working for yourself because whether you are a consultant, freelancer or the owner of a small business you have no one else to rely on for getting the message across to colleagues and employees, customers or clients, suppliers, service and information providers, bank managers, tax officers, accountants and auditors, government agencies and competitors. Before each marketing or sales pitch (whether it is to a potential client or the bank manager) it's worth ensuring that you know what message you want to communicate; who needs to receive that message; the best way to deliver the message; and, afterwards, that the message has been received and understood.

Some people seem to be very proficient at good communication in a workplace environment, but lose these skills in a home situation. If you are working at home, remember to use all your business skills in a positive way when you close the door of your office, just as you take the life skills from home into your work. If other members of your household are going to be answering your work phone calls from time to time, tell them in advance how you would like them to respond to clients or customers, and how you would prefer messages to be taken. Business contacts are unlikely to react negatively to knowing that you work from home, but it may be better to make this clear at the beginning of a relationship rather than let them assume you are in an office until they have a call answered by a small child.

Other ground rules you may want to establish early relate to the privacy of your work room, equipment, materials and data, when interruptions are and are not permissible, and levels of noise in the rest of the house during your working hours. If possible, make sure from the start that you are working as far as possible from the main living areas, that you have some sound-proofing or the ability to shut out noise, and that your phone, fax and e-mail lines are separate to those of the household. If you have to bring clients or customers into your home office, discuss your requirements with other members of the household in advance.

If you feel it is necessary to your business, spend as much as you can afford on a well-designed logo and some product literature; but this will be secondary in importance to your ability to network. Having or developing a wide range of contacts, and using those contacts for the benefit of your business, is a vital component of working for yourself. Once you have gained customers or clients keep in touch with them on a regular basis, whether you send them information about new products or services, special offers or even your own regular newsletter or information sheet (this could be sent out on e-mail). Increasing your sales to existing customers can be a much cheaper option than selling in to new prospects. Always ask clients for an evaluation of your service when a project is completed. This feedback will help you to keep your product focused, and satisfied customers may allow you to use them as referees as well as recommending you to others.

However, you should always try to broaden your market, and there are cost-free strategies for doing this. If you have a cutting edge product or service offer to write an article on the general area for a local newspaper, trade journal or other publication. Websites, radio even television stations might carry your story. One idea is to carry out some of your own research (you could add some additional questions on more general topics to your market research survey) and write up the results into a short report or press release. Whatever medium carries your material will certainly allow you to add your contact details at the end.

You could combine this approach with some paid advertising, which might feature a sales promotion such as coupons, price reductions, special offers or a competition with a free offer to the winner. You should also be able to get media coverage from a charitable donation, sports or community sponsorship or a story about how your business will enhance the local community by creating jobs or improving the quality of life. If you are an outgoing personality you might enjoy promoting yourself as a personality or expert in your field. Your home-working situation might even be one aspect of your business that is noteworthy, and its positive impact on your service something to emphasize in publicity materials.

Rob

Anthony told some of his golfing friends how Rob had helped him understand the software on his laptop, and they were interested in his skills. Two of them subsequently asked Rob to advise them on buying and setting up home PCs and another asked for some lessons on desktop publishing – all for an appropriate fee. This encouraged Rob to consider advertising his services locally, in the hope of building up enough work to pay his way through a coaching course at college. "I never thought I could make a living out of the two things I enjoy most – sport and computers. Maybe I should offer my dad a commission – no, on second thoughts he might be more impressed if I offered to pay some rent while I'm still living at home."

Exercise

Getting off to a flying start

Before you start trading, be sure of the following:

The definition of my 'offer' (service or product) is:	....
Its/my Unique Selling Point(s) is/are:	• .... • ....
My preliminary market research showed me I needed to adjust (eg product/ service/price/market):	• .... • ....
My registered trading name and website address are:	• .... • ....
My business plan includes the following (eg first year's income and expenditure/ first year's cash flow, market research analysis, bank loan):	• .... • .... • ....
My business advisors are (eg lawyer, accountant, book-keeper, financial/ insurance advisor):	• .... • .... • ....
My marketing/promotions plan includes (eg regular e-/mailshot, newsletter, media coverage, speaking engagements):	• .... • .... • ....
My ground rules for ensuring I maintain balance between my business and personal lives are:	• .... • .... • ....

Enacting your aims

Now for the final exercise in the Balance Model. In Chapter 4 you worked on the Negatives (barriers) and Commitments towards achieving your key Aims. Now that you know what the barriers are to you taking action (and how you might overcome them), and what is going to make you commit to achieving your Aims, it's time to take action.

Exercise

Answer the following questions and complete the form overleaf:

- What are the first moves you need to make to achieve this Aim?

- What is your timescale? Set yourself a realistic date for achieving the Aim.

- Think through who can help you achieve your Aim and how you can enlist their help.

- Whom will you be accountable to? Consider finding someone (who also wants to gain greater balance in their life) that you could work with on your project. A 'Balance Partner' can be an invaluable support with whom you could share Aims and check in with weekly or fortnightly to talk about your achievements or issues. A Balance Partner can also offer much needed advice or encouragement.

Enact your aims

WORK AIM 1:	
Will be achieved by	Date: ____ /____ /____
First moves will be:	• .... • .... • ....
People who can help are:	• .... • .... • ....
My Balance Partner is:	• ....
HOME AIM 1:	
Will be achieved by	Date: ____ /____ /____
First moves will be:	• .... • .... • ....
People who can help are:	• .... • .... • ....

CHAPTER 6

Resources

THIS CHAPTER COVERS:

- Personal time out.

- Staying healthy.

- Handling stress – flexibility, relaxation, breath control, focusing your mind.

- Financial fitness.

- Taking care of others.

- Back-up care.

- Still stuck? – further help.

Few of us manage to achieve a perfect work-life balance, and if we do it rarely lasts long. For a start, the balance is likely to shift constantly around changing work priorities, the people in your life, your personal interests, or be different according to whatever age or stage you are now at. Life, too, has a way of throwing spanners in the works at the most unexpected times. The secret to success is to build up your reserves – physical, emotional and financial – as a safety net. Having these in place will give you the confidence you need to move forward and deal with the unforeseen.

In this chapter we flag up some of the key areas to think about in terms of taking care of yourself and those around you.

Personal time out

You'll be more clear-headed and able to plan if you allow yourself regular 'time out' and space just to reflect and 'think outside the box'. What's your favourite escape? Some local haunt perhaps, such as a quiet table in a coffee bar or maybe a den of some kind at home – a corner that is your private space, a study, a basement or outside work-shop, your garden or the local park. It doesn't really matter what, the important thing is to find some place where you can take some time out to get lost in a book or a project, or simply to reflect and catch up with yourself. Or your escape might be a regular time each day or week when people know you can't be interrupted – exercise, listening to music, catching up with the papers, soaking in the bathtub or meditating.

Dave

> Dave had always wanted to get back to playing the guitar. However, he spent so much time at work that it seemed selfish to him to pursue this hobby and take time out from the family. But now that he and Karen were both managing to achieve more balance, Karen had surprised him by being supportive about him doing something different – anything as long as it wasn't work. In fact, she used Dave's idea to negotiate herself some personal space in return. Dave commented: "I'm now playing with some mates one evening a week, and Karen's doing a photography class on another evening when I make sure I'm home to babysit. We're both getting something out of this (even if it's not a joint activity) and feel good about helping one another get some time out."

There are also the bigger 'time outs' – holidays, weekend breaks, favourite sports fixtures in the year. Most people find it helps to make a habit of doing small things that are fun or rewarding at the personal level each week, but it may suit you to work flat out for a time and then look forward to a longer break. Build bigger treats into your schedule and budget. If you don't, they will always be squeezed out by everyone else's demands. When this happens there's a danger that you could eventually become resentful, de-energized or even in need of care yourself!

Ask yourself the following question: "What 'time out' activities to nurture myself would I enjoy doing most right now?"

Write in your Balance Book as many things as you can think of. Don't let practical barriers put you off – just capture all your ideas, large or small, on paper. When you've written down all you can, pick at least one small activity, that perhaps takes up little time – such as a walk around the block or buying a new CD or book to relax with – and schedule it into your Balance Diary every week for the next month.

Then ask yourself: "What else would I really enjoy in the longer term?"

Again, write as many ideas as come into your head in your Balance Book, and don't be limited by practicality or expense. These could include one-off or regular breaks, like a weekend away visiting a friend, or something longer term like taking up a new hobby. Choose which three activities most excite you and, for each, ask yourself:

- What's stopping me doing this right now?

- What is the first step to making it happen?

- What or who do I need to take into account in terms of resources or people?

- What, if anything, might I offer in return for getting this 'time out'?

Check your list of ideas in your Balance Book regularly and update it as new ideas occur to you. Cross off the ones you have done (or are doing) to gain a sense of achievement. At the start of each month or week ask yourself what you are doing to take care of yourself. You now have a useful list of ideas to fall back on!

Naomi

> Taking time out to see her family in Africa, Naomi realized how refreshing and energizing it was to take such a break. "The lab didn't fall apart while I was away – they knew where to get in touch with me if there was a real problem – and it was quite good for me and Ed to have some time apart, especially while the building work was going on." Naomi decided to make sure she did this at least twice a year in future, once on her own and once with Ed, if business allowed. "And when we have children this will mean they get to know their extended family because they'll see them on a regular basis. In future Ed will probably go skiing with friends while I'm away, which he'll enjoy (and I don't!)."

Staying healthy

Giving yourself some time and space is an important way to stay mentally healthy and alert. But what about your physical fitness? Do your job or hobbies keep you as fit as you'd like or, if not, what sort of shape would you like to be in five years from now? A healthy, well-balanced diet will help you operate at your best. What's more, with longer, more sedentary, lifestyles our bodies need to be kept in tune with regular exercise. Like any delicate mechanism expected to perform over time you deserve regular maintenance to prevent breakdown.

With so many more forms of exercise to choose from nowadays, there's probably a range of options nearby to suit your lifestyle, and the good news is that it need not cost a lot. Research shows that making a habit of regular exercise, such as walking each day, combined with a well-balanced diet and drinking plenty of water, is far more valuable than a short-lived binge at the gym (probably followed by a huge meal as a reward!). So don't think it is a question of all or nothing, focus instead on:

- What sort of routine would work for you and what are the good things about being active?

- What are the things you don't like about exercise, and what might be the cost of doing nothing?

Try to choose a variety of activities to maintain stamina, suppleness and strength. Go for things that are fun and help you feel good, that can be done regularly and fitted into your daily routine. It will help if they are convenient to your home or work, or can be done *en route*. Good, all-round activities are swimming, ball games, dancing and fitness classes. If getting out, or attending a regular class, is difficult there is a wide range of fitness videos on the market, from high-energy aerobics to gentle stretching exercises, such as yoga. Just doing 10 minutes each morning adds up to over five hours a month and makes a surprising difference to your sense of physical and mental well-being.

Think about what will keep you motivated – something you can do easily on your own each day, a class with others for support, or working one-to-one with a friend with the same aims, or a trainer? Most leisure centres have experts on hand who can suggest options to meet your needs and budget. Otherwise, try your health centre, adult education classes, community centre, YMCA or library. Look out for local health education or promotion units in the local press.

Anthony

> Anthony's doctor asked whether he took any regular exercise when he consulted her about his chest pains, and he realized he hadn't done so for ages. He went down to the local leisure centre with Della: "I admit I was dreading it, seeing all those fit guys lifting weights and working out, but the personal trainer down there was really helpful. He checked my fitness levels (a bit embarrassing, but he said he'd seen worse!) and then took me round all the exercise machines, told me what they did for each part of the body and then gave me a personal plan to follow." Anthony was now going in two evenings a week and whenever he could at weekends, and said he was really seeing a difference: "It's hard work, but even having my clothes fit better again gives me more confidence with clients – and Della's pleased too."

Handling stress

We've all been told how important it is to adapt and learn how to manage change. It would be more accurate to say that change is how we now manage. Just as many of us have learnt to use technology because of the benefits it can bring, it is also important for us to master ways of managing personal overload effectively.

In Chapter 4 we discussed ideas on how to work smarter to keep down your stress levels. There are other areas you can focus on to handle, and minimize, stress.

Physical flexibility

Simple stretches which work all the major joints and muscle groups help to release tension and restore physical balance. In the course of doing them you will release natural chemicals which help to promote a positive attitude and strengthen your immune system.

Performed regularly, these non-aerobic exercises increase suppleness and reduce tension pain in the back, shoulders, neck and head.

Relaxation

Purposeful relaxation of the body muscles, using techniques such as
visualization and auto-suggestion, can benefit the nervous system,
lungs and heart. The effectiveness of this simple practice is so great
that it is commonly prescribed by healthcare professionals to help treat
stress-related illness. Making a regular practice of relaxation exercises
will help you to sleep better and gain a sense of calm and control which
will lead to better all-round health.

Breath control

The impact of stress is often accelerated and intensified by shallow
and irregular breathing patterns which can activate the body's
natural defence mechanism and add to your sense of anxiety.
Learning to relax your breathing can therefore be a powerful preven-
tive force and a natural antidote for stress. In addition, correct, deep
breathing is vital as 70% of your body's waste products are eliminated
through exhalation. Shallow, fast breathing means waste products
are circulating in your system, leading to sluggishness and toxic
build-up.

Focusing the mind

It is easy to have a sense of overload when you face a seemingly endless
list of things to do and deadlines to meet. Instead of trying to reach an
end (that is never likely to come), practise the art of focusing on the
present moment and learn to trust your ability to manage. Techniques
such as meditation will help, and it is also important to consider your
physical environment. Are you sitting comfortably? Is your posture

good? If you have to concentrate on something specific, what interruptions are you tolerating?

Your working environment may not always be perfect but think about
what could be improved or ways to screen out interruptions at certain
times in the day when you want to be more focused.

Yoga, relaxation, meditation, massage, biofeedback, psychological
conditioning, music, physical exercise – even just a walk round the
block – all are recommended as stress relief therapies. Finding a low-
maintenance programme to suit your lifestyle will produce high, measurable outcomes in improved health, productivity and sense of general
well-being. Just as there is a growing range of exercise options in most
areas, guidance and classes on managing stress are growing to meet
demand. If there are no courses nearby, or your time is limited, you
should find plenty of books and tapes at your local library or bookstore
to help you get started at home.

Sarah

> Sarah thought she would be the oldest person there when she signed up
> for a yoga class, but found there were quite a few people of her age and
> that she could do most of the exercises for beginners. "We start the class
> with some stretches; I've now started doing them when I get up in the
> morning and feel a lot less creaky in the joints. I do some deep breathing
> in the car while Tom's driving us to work, which seems to be very calming
> at the start of the day. If I can't sleep at night I go through one of the
> relaxation exercises we do in class. You lie flat on your back and say to
> yourself 'My feet are warm and relaxed', then you work all the way up your
> muscles and joints. By the time I get to my neck and head I'm half asleep
> anyway, but I always sleep well afterwards."

Financial fitness

Keeping financially fit and building up some kind of reserve is as important for your peace of mind and sense of well-being as staying physically on form. If you are living outside your means, and not putting any money aside for times when you may want or need to take a break from work, then you will have little sense of choice or control over the kind of work-life balance you are aiming for in the future.

Whatever your income, try to get into the habit of having a surplus at the end of each month. Aim to set aside at least 10% of your earnings for future contingencies – eg retraining, investment in equipment if you decide to set up on your own, a career break or a longer-term reduction in work towards retirement.

If you are not already living within your means, and find it hard to identify where savings could be made, try running through your expenditure with a friend, personal coach or independent financial advisor. What could you do to change the situation? Could you cut any unnecessary expenses, go out without your credit card, change your lifestyle, find ways to justify a pay rise from your employer? Facing up to reality may not be much fun at first, but gaining more control in this area of your life will make a huge difference to your energy levels.

Jonathan

Jonathan found that taking control of one area of his life gave him the motivation to do it in others. Once he had spoken to his team about not covering for them all the time, and started working better hours, he thought about planning his spending better so he could pay a dog-walker for Max, or at least have an emergency fund in case his neighbour got sick. His economy was simply to buy one less CD a week than he would normally allow himself: "It wasn't a lot, but after three months of putting that money into a savings account I felt a lot safer about facing unexpected problems."

Karen

When Karen got her first pay her initial impulse was to go and blow it on some new clothes for herself and the kids, especially as she got a discount on the ones she bought from her employer. "But then I thought about our debts and I decided that half of everything I earned would go into paying off the loan and the other half would go into a savings account for the kids' futures. That way, if either of them take up an expensive hobby or they want to go to college there's something to start them off."

Taking care of others

Taking good care of yourself is essential if you are to sustain a caring role for others. Also, if you are responsible for organizing care for children or other dependants, it is vital that you make the best possible choice in terms of care provider.

Quite what those choices are will depend largely on where you live. But wherever that is you are unlikely to be alone in seeking information about providers. With so many people now combining work with caring responsibilities you should be able to access a range of local resources to help you. As a first step, check out your local council, health centre, library and phone directory for childcare, eldercare and specialist providers. You may also find relevant voluntary organizations in your area who can provide guidance. If you work for a large employer, you may find that they can help with this kind of information or can put you in touch with a specialist referral service.

Some will have on-site or subsidised childcare; a few even cater for eldercare requirements. New websites are being created all the time in this field, so if you have access to the internet you could do a search using relevant key words. For children's services, search under 'childcare' or 'daycare'; for adult dependants try 'caregivers', 'eldercare' or 'ageing'.

Don't forget local word-of-mouth as this can turn up information on your doorstep; but always check out personal recommendations and follow up references. Professional carers who are insured and have a basic standard of quality control will most likely be registered in some way, either by the local council or a professional association, and it makes sense to check this out before entering into any agreement.

Childcare options	Suitable for pre-school children		Suitable for schoolage children	
	Full time	Part time	Term time	Holidays
Childminder	Yes	Yes	Yes	Yes
Out of school scheme/kids' club	No	No	Yes	Yes
Day nursery	Yes	Yes	No	No
Nursery classes	No	Yes	No	No
Playgroups	Yes	Yes	No	No
Nanny	Yes	Yes	Yes	Yes
Au Pair/mother's help	No	Yes	Yes	Yes
Holiday play scheme	No	No	No	Yes

Demand for good quality care far outstrips supply so it is a good idea to start looking at your options well before you actually need them and, if necessary, putting your name down on any waiting lists.

Della

Della's sister lived close to their parents and had recently told Della that though they were well, their father's eyesight was getting worse and he might not be able to go on driving, and their mother's arthritis was making the cleaning hard for her. Teresa had spoken to the local council about what was available in terms of home help, and was paying a neighbour to do some shopping errands for them. That seemed so sensible to Della that she spoke to one of Anthony's parents' neighbours, who always seemed friendly. "She was really pleased to think she could both help and earn a bit of extra money; she's going to pop in on them every morning, do a bit of shopping and help his mum with her ironing." Anthony's parents were happy about that and it was making a real difference to Della not to have to worry about them every day. Anthony planned to talk to his brother about checking out nursing homes, what was available and the cost. "They don't need it yet, but there might be a waiting list for the good ones and it's better to be prepared."

Back-up care

However good the care arrangements you make, it is wise to have a back-up plan in case of emergencies. If you work for a large employer the chances are they will have some form of policy regarding leave for family emergencies. Check out your staff handbook or seek guidance from the HR department about what to do in cases of emergency, and make sure that if you have a partner they are familiar with their employer's policies too. Sound out your direct line manager and, if it is possible, suggest a flexible agreement which allows for some give and take on both sides in case of emergencies.

Discuss with your partner or other primary carers how you will divide up care responsibilities in an emergency. Will you take it in turns or review each situation as it arises? If you have to take time out from work can this be made up later or will you lose holiday or pay for that day? Who else can you turn to in an emergency? Does your regular provider have any suggestions or back-up, or do you have a relative, close friend or neighbour who can step in at short notice? It is a good idea to have a couple of contingency plans and contact numbers at your finger tips in case of emergencies. Keep the details readily to hand, on a kitchen notice board or in the back of your diary for quick reference should the need ever arise.

Still stuck?

Despite best intentions, we sometimes find ourselves going round and round in circles, unable to move forward or apply any new ideas, however promising. Talking candidly to a friend or partner may help, especially if there is a reciprocal agreement to give one another 'listening time'. You could also consider seeking outside help, from a mentor, coach, counsellor or therapist.

Mentors

A mentor is someone who has probably experienced some of the things that you are currently going through and can give you both encouragement and guidance to help you move forward. You could seek out a friend or work colleague to be an informal mentor for an agreed period of time, or ask at your workplace or college about organized mentoring schemes.

Coaches

Coaching is a partnership between coach and client that provides the structure, support and focus to help you identify and achieve personal or business goals. Working either face to face, by phone or via e-mail, coaches can offer specialist experience in life transitions, career planning, business or executive development; however, the main focus is on helping the client to set achievable goals of their own design. Coaches are accredited, and can be found, via the International Coach Federation (www.coachfederation.org).

Christopher

"After I'd been out of work for a few months, my wife started to get worried about me and thought I was drifting. I'd vaguely talked about retraining or changing direction, but couldn't get myself organized to do anything. My wife Joanna had had her own coach for about a year; she had started having coaching when our daughter was very young and she felt overwhelmed by looking after her and maintaining her career. Anyway, she got me to agree that I'd give it a go if she organized some coaches to contact me. I wasn't very impressed by the idea of talking to someone I'd never met, but within a week I had received about 12 e-mails from people who all sounded nice and helpful. I decided to go with Nick, who had some similar life experience to me and I talked to him every week for about three months; to my surprise it really helped. The weekly phone calls gave me a sense of purpose and accountability (as we set my goals each week), and an objective viewpoint. Within two months I'd decided – with Jo, of course – that what I really wanted to do was build us a house and then use that experience to work in that field. We can't move for another 18 months, so I'm still looking for an IT job, but I now have a longer-term plan and some steps towards getting there. I still talk to Nick about once a month to get his input on anything in my life, personal or professional. Even though I've never met him I think of him as a friend and support."

Counselling and therapy

If you suffer from any addictions, low self-esteem, relationship issues, depression or other mental health problems that are stopping you from moving forward there is a huge range of individual or group counselling and therapy to choose from. Ask your doctor or health clinic for guidance or find out what is available locally through your library. Alternatively, you could do some background research using the internet. Key words to search under are 'counselling', 'cognitive' or 'analytic' therapy, 'family', 'couple', 'sexual' and 'systemic' therapy, 'neuro-linguistic programming', 'psychoanalysis' and 'psychotherapy'.

Further reading

Some other books you might find helpful include:

Be Your Own Life Coach, Fiona Harrold, Hodder & Stoughton, 2000

Be Your Own Mentor, Sheila Wellington, Random House, 2001

Get Everything Done and Still Have Time to Play, Mark Forster, Hodder & Stoughton, 2000

How To Get What You Want And Want What You Have, John Gray, Vermillion, 1999

Living Your Best Life, Laura Berman Fortgang, HarperCollins, 2001

Managing Workplace Stress, Susan Cartwright, Cary L Cooper, Sage Publications, 1997

The 7 Habits of Highly Effective People, Stephen R Covey, Simon & Schuster, 1990

Slowing Down to the Speed of Life, Richard Carlson and Joseph Bailey, Hodder & Stoughton, 1998

Successful Stress Management in a Week, Cary Cooper and Alison Straw, Hodder & Stoughton, 1993

Three Easy Steps to the Job You Want, Malcolm Hornby, Prentice Hall, 2000

What Colour Is Your Parachute 2002, N Bolles, Ten Speed Press

Who Moved My Cheese?, Dr Spencer Johnson, Vermillion, 1998

Your Mind At Work, Richard Israel, Helen Whitten and Cliff Shaffran, Kogan Page, 2000

Your Personal Survival Guide to the 21st Century, Roy Sheppard, Centre Publications, 1998